The Family and Individual Development

by the same author

CLINICAL NOTES ON DISORDERS OF CHILDHOOD

THE CHILD AND THE FAMILY

THE CHILD AND THE OUTSIDE WORLD

COLLECTED PAPERS: THROUGH PAEDIATRICS TO PSYCHO-ANALYSIS

THE CHILD, THE FAMILY, AND THE OUTSIDE WORLD (*paperback*)

THE MATURATIONAL PROCESS AND THE
FACILITATING ENVIRONMENT

The Family
and Individual Development

D. W. Winnicott
F.R.C.P. (LOND.)

TAVISTOCK PUBLICATIONS
LONDON and NEW YORK

First published in 1965 by
Tavistock Publications Limited
11 New Fetter Lane, London EC4P 4EE
First published as a Social Science Paperback 1968
Reprinted five times
Reprinted 1986

Published in the USA by
Tavistock Publications
in association with Methuen, Inc.
29 West 35th Street, New York NY 10001

ISBN 0 422 72370 3

Printed in Great Britain by
J. W. Arrowsmith Ltd, Bristol

Contents

v

Preface

Here I have gathered together papers given during the past decade, mostly to groups of social workers. The central topic of the book is the family, and the development of social groups out of this first natural group. I have included various attempts to state and restate the theory of the emotional growth of the individual human child, and my justification for this is that the structure of the family arises to a large extent out of the tendencies towards organization in the individual personality.

The family has a clearly defined position at the place where the developing child meets the forces that operate in society. The prototype of this interaction is to be found in the original infant-mother relationship in which, in an extremely complex way, the world represented by the mother is helping or hindering the inherited tendency of the infant to grow. It is this idea that is developed in the course of this collection of papers, although each was designed to meet what seemed to be the needs of the groups concerned at a specific time and place.

ACKNOWLEDGEMENTS

I wish once more to thank my secretary, Mrs Joyce Coles, for her patient and accurate work.

To Mr M. Masud Khan I am grateful for his advice and for his work on the index.

Acknowledgement of debt is also due to the following editors, publishers, and organizations for permission to publish material that has already appeared in print: the Editor of the *New Era in Home and School*; the Editor of the *Nursing Times*; the Editor of *New Society*; the Editor of the *British Journal of Psychiatric Social Work*; the Editor of the *Medical Press*; the Editor of *Human Relations*; the Editor of the *Canadian Medical Association Journal*; Butterworth & Co. (Publishers) Ltd; the British Broadcasting Corporation.

A list of original sources is given overleaf.

D. W. WINNICOTT, F.R.C.P.

ACKNOWLEDGEMENTS

1 Published in the *Medical Press*, March 1958.

2 Lecture given to the Association of Workers for Maladjusted Children, April 1960 (Rewritten 1964).

4 BBC broadcast, March 1960.

5 BBC broadcast, June 1962.

6 Lecture given at Goldsmith's College, October 1957; to the Association of Child Care Officers, May 1958; and at McGill University, October 1960; subsequently published in the *Canadian Medical Association Journal*, April 1961.

7 Lecture given at the Family Service Units Caseworkers' Study Weekend, October 1958.

8 Lecture to the Association of Child Care Officers, February 1960.

9 Lecture to the Association of Psychiatric Social Workers, November 1959; subsequently published in the *British Journal of Psychiatric Social Work*, vol. 6, no. 1, 1961.

10 Based on a lecture given to the Senior Staff of the London County Council Children's Department, February 1961; subsequently published in *New Era in Home and School*, October 1962; and in an altered form, entitled 'Struggling through the Doldrums', in *New Society*, 25 April 1963.

11 Lecture to the Society for Psychosomatic Research, November 1960.

12 Part of Chapter 14 in *Modern Trends in Paediatrics* (Second Series), edited by A. Holzel & J. P. M. Tizard (London: Butterworth, 1958).

13 Lecture given at a course organized by the Association of Supervisors of Midwives; subsequently published in the *Nursing Times*, 17 and 24 May 1957.

14 Lecture given at a course for midwives organized by the Royal College of Midwives, November 1957.

15 Lecture to the Association of London County Council Child Welfare Officers, October 1959.

16 Lecture to the Nursery School Association, July 1950.

17 Lecture to the Association of Workers for Maladjusted Children, April 1955.

18 Published in *Human Relations*, vol. 3, no. 2, June 1950.

To
Clare

Part 1

1

The First Year of Life
Modern Views on the Emotional Development

INTRODUCTION

A great deal happens in the first year of the life of the human infant: emotional development starts at the beginning; in a study of the evolution of the personality and character it is not possible to ignore the events of the first days and hours (even the last part of the prenatal life when the infant is post-mature); and even birth experience may be significant.

The world has kept turning in spite of our ignorance in these matters simply because there is something about the mother of a baby, something which makes her particularly suited to the protection of her infant in this stage of vulnerability, and which makes her able to contribute positively to the baby's positive needs. The mother is able to fulfil this role if she feels secure; if she feels loved in her relation to the infant's father and to her family; and also feels accepted in the widening circles around the family which constitute society.

If we like, we may continue to leave the task of infant care to the mother, whose capacity does not rest on knowledge but comes from a feeling attitude which she acquires as the pregnancy advances, and which she gradually loses as the infant grows up out of her. However, there are reasons why we may profit from a study of what goes on in the early stages of the development of the infant personality. For instance, as doctors and nurses we may need to interfere with the infant-mother relationship in order to deal with the infant's physical abnormalities, and we ought to know what we are interfering with. Moreover, the physical study of infancy has given rich rewards in the past fifty years, and it might well be that a similar interest in emotional development would produce rewards even more rich. A third reason would be that a proportion of mothers and fathers cannot provide good-enough conditions at the time of the infant's birth, on account of social, family, or personal illness, and then doctors and nurses are expected to be able to understand and to treat, even to prevent; just as they often have power to do in cases of physical disease. The paediatrician will increasingly need to be as well orientated on the emotional as he is at the present time on the physical side

3

of the map of infant growth.

There is yet a fourth reason for the study of early emotional growth: it is often possible to detect and to diagnose emotional disorder in infancy, even during the first year of life. Clearly, the right time for the treatment of such disorder is the time of its inception, or as near to it as possible. But I will not pursue this theme at this point.

Nor will I make reference to physical abnormality or physical ill health; or to mental growth in terms of developmental tendency, affected by hereditary factors. For present purposes the infant may be assumed to be sound in body and *potentially* sound in mind; and what I want to discuss is the meaning of this potentiality. What is potential at birth, and, of this, what has become actual at one year? I assume, too, the existence of a mother, a mother who is healthy enough to behave naturally as a mother. Owing to the extreme emotional dependence of the infant, the development or life of an infant cannot be discussed apart from infant care.

I have set down below a series of statements, each briefly expanded. These condensed observations will perhaps indicate to those concerned with the care of the infant the fact that the emotional development of the first year of life comprises the foundation of the mental health of the human individual.

INNATE TENDENCY TOWARDS DEVELOPMENT

In psychological matters there is a tendency towards development which is innate, and which corresponds to the growth of the body and the gradual development of functions. Just as a baby usually sits at about five or six months, and walks somewhere near the first birthday, and perhaps uses two or three words at that time, so there is a process of evolution in emotional development. However, we do not witness this natural growth unless conditions are good enough, and part of our difficulty is the description of the good-enough conditions. In what follows it will be necessary to take for granted the ontogenetic process, and the neurophysiological basis of behaviour.

DEPENDENCE

The great change that is noticed in the first year of life is in the direction of independence. Independence is something that is achieved out of dependence, but it is necessary to add that dependence is achieved out of what might be called double dependence. At the very beginning there is an absolute dependence on the physical and emotional environment. In the earliest stage there is no vestige of an awareness of this dependence, and for this reason the dependence is absolute. Gradually dependence becomes to some extent known to the infant who, in consequence, acquires the capacity for letting the environment know when attention is needed. Clinically there is found a very gradual progress towards independence, with dependence and even double dependence always reappearing. The mother is able to adapt herself to the varying – and growing – needs of her infant in this as in other respects. By one year old, the infant has become able to keep alive the idea of the mother and also of the child care to which he or she is accustomed, to keep alive this idea for a certain length of time, perhaps ten minutes, perhaps an hour, perhaps longer.

What is found at one year, however, is extremely variable, variable not only from one infant to another but also in any one infant. The achievement of a degree of independence may quite normally be lost and regained over and over again, and often an infant may return to dependence after being markedly independent at one year.

This journey from double dependence to dependence and from dependence to independence is something that is not only an expression of the innate tendency of the infant to grow; this growth cannot take place unless a very sensitive adaptation is made by someone to the infant's needs. It happens that the infant's mother is better than anyone else at performing this most delicate and constant task; she is more suitable than anyone else because she is the one who is most likely to be quite naturally and without resentment devoted to this cause.

INTEGRATION

From the beginning it is possible for the observer to see that an infant is already a human being, a unit. By the age of one year most infants have in fact achieved the status of an individual. In other words, the personality has become integrated. This is not of course true all the time, but at certain moments and over certain periods and in certain relationships the infant of one year is a whole person. But integration is not something that can be taken for granted; it is something that must develop gradually in every individual infant. It is not a matter simply of neurophysiology, since for this process to take place there must be certain environmental conditions, actually, those which are best provided by the infant's own mother.

Integration appears gradually out of a primary unintegrated state. At the beginning the infant is made up of a number of motility phases and sensory perceptions. It is almost certain that rest for the infant means a return to an unintegrated state. A return to unintegration is not necessarily frightening to the infant because of a sense of security that is given by the mother. Sometimes security means simply being held well. Both physically and in more subtle ways the mother or the environment holds the infant together, and

5

unintegration can take place along with reintegration without the development of anxiety.

Integration appears to be linked with the more definite emotional or affective experiences, such as rage, or the excitement of a feeding situation. Gradually, as integration becomes a settled fact and the infant becomes more and more knit together into a unit, so does the undoing of what has been gained become disintegration rather than unintegration. Disintegration is painful.

The degree to which integration has taken place at one year is variable: some infants at this age are already in possession of a strong personality, a self with the personal characteristics exaggerated; others, at the other extreme, have not by the first birthday acquired so definite a personality, and are very much dependent on continuous care.

PERSONALIZATION

The infant at one year is firmly living in the body. The psyche and the soma have come to terms with each other. The neurologist would say that body-tone is satisfactory, and would describe the infant's coordination as good. This state of affairs, in which the psyche and the soma are intimately related to each other, develops out of the initial stages in which the immature psyche (although based on body functioning) is not closely bound to the body and to the life of the body. When a reasonable degree of adaptation to the needs of the infant is provided, this gives the best possible chance for an early establishment of a firm relationship between the psyche and the soma. Where there is a failure of adaptation, so there is a tendency for the psyche to develop an existence that is only loosely related to bodily experience, the result being that physical frustrations are not always felt with full intensity.

Even in health, the infant of one year is firmly rooted to the body only at certain times. The psyche of a normal infant may lose touch with the body, and there may be phases in which it is not easy for the infant to come suddenly back into the body, for instance, when waking from deep sleep. Mothers know this, and they gradually wake an infant before lifting him or her, so as not to cause the tremendous screaming of panic which can be brought about by a change of position of the body at a time when the psyche is absent from it. Associated clinically with this absence of the psyche there may be phases of pallor, times when the infant is sweating and perhaps very cold, and there may be vomiting. At this stage the mother can think her infant is dying, but by the time the doctor has arrived there has been so complete a return to normal health that the doctor is unable to understand why the mother was alarmed. Naturally, the general practitioner knows more about this syndrome than the consultant.

MIND AND PSYCHE-SOMA

By the age of one year the infant has quite clearly developed the beginnings of a mind. Mind means something quite distinct from psyche. The psyche is related to the soma and to body functioning, but the mind depends on the existence and functioning of those parts of the brain that are developed at a later stage (in phylogenesis) than the parts that are concerned with the primitive psyche. (It is the mind which gradually makes it possible for the infant to wait for the feed because of the noises that indicate that a feed will be forthcoming. This is a crude example of the use of the mind.)

It could be said that at the beginning the mother must adapt almost exactly to the infant's needs in order that the infant personality shall develop without distortion. She is able to fail in her adaptation, however, and to fail increasingly, and this is because the infant's mind and the infant's intellectual processes are able to account for and so to allow for failures of adaptation. In this way the mind is allied to the mother and takes over part of her function. In the care of an infant the mother is dependent on the infant's intellectual processes, and it is these that enable her gradually to re-acquire a life of her own.

There are, of course, other ways in which the mind develops. It is a function of mind to catalogue events, and to store up memories and classify them. Because of the mind the infant is able to make use of time as a measurement and also to measure space. The mind also relates cause and effect.

It would be instructive to compare conditioning in relation to the mind and to the psyche, and such a study might throw light on the differences between these two phenomena which are so regularly confused the one with the other.

Obviously there is a very great variation from one infant to another in the capacity of the mind to help the mother in her management. Most mothers are able to adapt to each infant's good or poor mental capacity, to go as fast or as slow as the infant. It is only too easy, however, for a quick mother to get out of step with one of her children who happens to be limited in intellectual capacity; and the quick child is also liable to be out of touch with a slow mother.

At a certain age the child becomes able to allow for the mother's characteristics, and so to be relatively independent of her incapacity to adapt to her infant's needs, but perhaps not before the first birthday.

FANTASY AND IMAGINATION

Characteristic of the human infant is fantasy, which may be thought of as the imaginative elaboration of physical function. Fantasy rapidly becomes infinitely complex, but at the start it is presumably restricted in quantity. By

7

direct observation it is not possible to assess the fantasy of a small infant, but play of any kind indicates the existence of fantasy.

It is convenient to trace the development of fantasy by making an artificial classification:

(i) Simple elaboration of function.

(ii) Separation out into: anticipation, experience, and memory.

(iii) Experience in terms of the memory of experience.

(iv) Localization of fantasy within or without the self, with interchange and constant enrichment of each from the other.

(v) Construction of a personal or inner world, with sense of responsibility for what exists and what goes on there.

(vi) Separation out of consciousness from that which is unconscious. The unconscious includes aspects of the psyche which are so primitive that they never become conscious, and also aspects of the psyche or of the mental functioning which become inaccessible in defence against anxiety (called the repressed unconscious).

There is a considerable degree of evolution of fantasy within the first year. It is important to remember that although this (as all other growth) takes place as a part of the natural tendency towards growth, evolution is stunted or distorted except under certain conditions. The nature of these conditions can be studied, and even stated.

PERSONAL (INNER) REALITY

The inner world of the individual has become a definite organization by the end of the first year. Positive elements are derived from the patterns of personal experience, especially of instinctual experience, interpreted in a personal way, and ultimately based on the individual's inborn inherited characteristics (in so far as they have appeared at this early date). This sample of the world that is personal to the infant is becoming organized according to complex mechanisms which have as their purpose:

(i) the preservation of what is felt to be 'good' – that is to say, acceptable and strengthening to the self (ego);

(ii) the isolation of what is felt to be 'bad' – that is to say, unacceptable, persecutory, or injected from external reality without acceptance (trauma);

(iii) the preservation of an area in the personal psychic reality in which objects have living interrelationships, exciting, and even aggressive, as well as affectionate.

By the end of the first year there are even the beginnings of secondary defences which deal with the breakdown of the primary organization; for instance, a general damping down of all inner life, with clinical manifestation in the depressed mood; or a massive projection into external reality of inner world elements, with clinical manifestation in an attitude towards the world that is tinged with patanoia. A very common clinical manifestation of the latter would be food fads – for example, suspicion of skin on milk.

The infant's view of the world external to the self is largely based on the pattern of the personal inner reality, and it should be noted that the actual behaviour of the environment towards an infant is to some extent affected by the infant's positive and negative expectations.

INSTINCTUAL LIFE

At first the instinctual life of the infant is based on the alimentary functioning. Hand and mouth interests predominate, but gradually excretory functions make their contribution. At a certain age, perhaps five months, the infant begins to be able to connect excreting with feeding, and faeces and urine with oral intake. Along with this comes the beginning of the acquisition of a personal inner world, which therefore tends to be localized in the belly. From this simple pattern there is a spreading out of psyche-soma experience to include the whole of the body functioning.

Breathing gets caught up in whatever predominates at the time, so that it may be associated now with intake and now with output. An important characteristic of breathing is that, except during crying, it lays bare a continuity of inner and outer, that is to say, a failure of defences.

All functions tend to have an orgastic quality in that they each in their own way contain a phase of local excitement and preparation, a climax with general bodily involvement, and a period of aftermath.

The anal function acquires more and more importance, so that it may predominate over oral function. The orgasm of excretion is normally an excretory orgasm, but in certain circumstances the anus may become an accepting organ, and gather to itself some of the importance of oral function and intake. Naturally, anal manipulations increase the likelihood of such a complication.

In both male and female infants urinary excretion is liable to be orgastic, and correspondingly exciting and satisfactory. Orgastic satisfaction, however, depends to a considerable extent on correct timing. Efforts to train infants in regard to their excretory processes, if successful, rob the infant of the physical satisfactions that belong to the era of infancy, and the consequences of training instituted too early are immense, often disastrous.

Genital excitement is not of prime importance during the first year of life. Nevertheless, in boys there may be erection and in girls vaginal activities, both occurring mainly in association with excited feeding or with the idea of feeding. Vaginal activities are liable to be roused by anal manipulations. Phallic erection begins, in the first year, to have an importance of its own, and clitoris excitement has a corresponding position. By the first birthday, however, it is not usual for the girl baby to have begun to envy the boy his genital, an organ which (as compared with the clitoris or the vulva) is obvious when at rest and still more obvious when roused. This discrepancy will tend to give rise to swank and envy in the next year or two. (Genital function and fantasy do not reach the position of dominance over the ingestive and excretory functions until the period roughly outlined by the ages of two to five.)

During the first year the instinctual experiences carry the infant's rapidly growing capacity for relating to objects, a capacity which culminates in a love relationship as between two whole persons, baby and mother. The triangular relationship, with its specific enrichment and complications, is becoming a new factor in the infant's life at about the time of the first birthday, but it does not reach its full status until the child is of toddler age, and until the time of dominance of the genital over the various types of alimentary instinctual functioning and fantasy.

The reader will easily recognize in this account Freud's theory of infantile sexuality, which was the first contribution from psycho-analysis to the understanding of the emotional life of infants. The whole idea of an instinctual life in infancy roused an immense reaction in public feeling, but it is now generally recognized that this theory is the central theme in the psychology of normal infancy as well as in the study of the roots of psychoneurosis.

OBJECT RELATIONSHIPS

The infant at one year is at times a whole person related to whole persons. This achievement has developed gradually, and only becomes a fact when conditions are sufficiently good.

The early state is a relationship to part-objects – for instance, the baby related to a breast, the mother not being a feature even although the baby may 'know' the mother at moments of affectionate contact. It is the gradual integration of the infant's personality into a unit that makes it possible for the part-object (breast, etc.) to be felt by the infant to be part of a whole person, and this aspect of development brings in its train specific anxieties. These will be referred to under capacity for concern (p. 13 below).

Along with the recognition of the whole object comes the beginning of a sense of dependence, and therefore the beginning of the need for independence. Also, the perception of the dependability of the mother makes possible the existence of the quality of dependability in the infant.

At an earlier stage, before the infant operates as a unit, object relationships are of the nature of a union of part with part. There is an extreme degree of variability in respect of the existence at any one stage of a whole self which is available for experiencing, and for retaining the memory of experiences.

SPONTANEITY

Instinctual impulse creates a situation which either proceeds to satisfaction, or else fizzles out in a diffuse dissatisfaction or general discomfort of both psyche and soma. There is a time for the satisfaction of an impulse, a climax to be matched with actual experience. Satisfactions are of immense importance to the infant in the first year of life, and it is only gradually that each infant becomes able to allow for being kept waiting. What is asked, of course, is that the infant shall give up spontaneity in favour of compliance with the needs of those who are caring for the infant. We sometimes ask of infants more than we can achieve ourselves.

Spontaneity is thus threatened by two sets of factors:

   (i) by the mother's wish to free herself from the bondage of motherhood, and this may be overlaid by the mother's mistaken idea that she must train her infant early in order to produce a 'good' child;

  (ii) by the development by complex mechanisms of a restriction of spontaneity from within the infant (the establishment of a superego).

It is this development of control from within that forms the only true basis for morality, and morality starts even in this first year of the individual's life. It starts as a result of crude fears of retaliation, and continues as a curbing of the instinctual life of the infant (who is becoming established as a person with a sense of concern); it protects the objects of love from the full blast of primitive love, primitive love being ruthless and aiming only at satisfaction of instinctual impulse.

At first the mechanics of self-control are crude like the impulses themselves, and the strictness of the mother helps by being less brutal and more human; for a mother can be defied, but the inhibition of an impulse from within is liable to be total. The strictness of mothers has an unexpected significance, therefore, in that it produces compliance gently and gradually, and saves the infant from the fierceness of self-control. By natural evolution, if the external conditions remain favourable, the infant sets up a 'human' internal strictness, and so manages self-control without too great a loss of that spontaneity which alone makes life worth living.

CREATIVE CAPACITY

The subject of spontaneity leads on naturally to the subject of the creative impulse, that which (as nothing else) proves to the child that he or she is alive.

The innate creative impulse withers unless it is met by external reality ('realized'). Each infant must re-create the world, but this is only possible if, bit by bit, the world arrives at the moments of the infant's creative activity. The infant reaches out and the breast is there, and the breast is created. The success of this operation depends on the sensitive adaptation the mother is making to her infant's needs, especially at the beginning.

From this there is a natural progression to the individual infant's creation of the whole world of external reality, and to the continuous creating which at first needs an audience and which then eventually creates even the audience. The painful early stages of this life process belong to early infancy, and to the mother's capacity to produce the reality sample at more or less the right moment. She can do this because she is identified with her infant, temporarily, to an extreme degree.

MOTILITY – AGGRESSION

Motility is a feature of the live foetus, and the movements of a premature infant in an incubator presumably give a picture of the infant in the womb near term. Motility is the precursor of aggression, which is a term that develops meaning as the infant grows. A special instance of aggression appears in the hand-grasp and in chewing activities which later become biting. In health a large proportion of the aggressive potential becomes fused in with the infant's instinctual experiences, and with the pattern of the individual infant's relationships. Good-enough environmental conditions are necessary for this development to take place.

In ill health only a small proportion of the aggressive potential becomes fused in with the erotic life, and the infant is then burdened with impulses that make no sense. These eventually lead to destructiveness in the relationship to objects, or, worse, form the basis of activity that is entirely senseless, as, for instance, a convulsion. There is a liability for this unfused aggression to appear in the form of an expectation or attack. This is one way in which there may be a pathology of emotional development, evident from a very early stage, and eventually showing as a psychiatric disorder. Such a disorder may, obviously, have paranoid features.

The aggressive potential is extremely variable because it depends not only on innate factors but also on the chance of environmental mishap; for instance, certain kinds of difficult birth can profoundly affect the state of the infant that is just born; and even being born normally may perhaps have some features that are traumatic for the infant's immature psyche, which knows no other defence except that of reacting, and so temporarily ceasing to exist in its own right.

CAPACITY FOR CONCERN

Somewhere in the second half of the first year of the normal infant's life there appears evidence of a capacity to be concerned, or an ability to experience guilt feeling. Here is a highly complex state of affairs, one that depends on the integration of the infant personality into a unit, and on the infant's acceptance of responsibility for the total fantasy of what belongs to the instinctual moment. For this highly sophisticated achievement the continued presence of the mother (or her substitute) is a necessary precondition, and the attitude of the mother must contain the element of being ready so see and accept the infant's immature efforts to contribute, that is to say, to repair, to love constructively. This important stage in the emotional development has been studied in great detail by Melanie Klein, in her extension of psycho-analytic (Freudian) theory to cover the origins of the personal guilt sense, and of the urge to act in a constructive way, and to give. In this way potency (and the acceptance of potency) has one of its roots in the emotional development that takes place before (as well as after) the first birthday.

POSSESSIONS

By the age of one year, infants have usually acquired one or several soft objects, teddies, rag dolls, etc., which are important to them. (Some boys prefer hard objects.) Obviously these objects stand for part-objects, notably for the breast, and only gradually do they stand for babies and for mother or father.

It is very interesting to study the infant's use of the very first object adopted, perhaps a bit of wool from a blanket, or a napkin, or a silk scarf. This object can become vitally important, and can have value as an object intermediate between the self and the outside world. Typically a child can be seen going to sleep clutching such an object (called by me a 'transitional object'), and at the same time sucking two fingers or a thumb, and perhaps stroking the upper lip or the nose. The pattern is personal to the child, and this pattern, which appears at the time of going to sleep, or at times of loneliness, sadness, anxiety, may persist to late childhood or even to adult life. This is all part of normal emotional development.

These phenomena (that I call transitional) appear to form the basis of the whole cultural life of the adult human being.

Severe deprivation may lead to a loss of the capacity to use the well-tried technique, with resulting restlessness and sleeplessness. Clearly the thumb in the mouth and the rag doll in the hand simultaneously symbolize a part of the self and a part of the environment.

Here is an opportunity for the observer to study the origins of affectionate behaviour, which is important (if for no other reason) because the loss of the capacity to be affectionate is a characteristic of the older 'deprived child', who clinically displays an antisocial tendency and is a candidate for delinquency.

LOVE

As the infant grows, the meaning of the word 'love' alters, or the meaning gathers to itself new elements:

(i) Love means existing, breathing, and being alive, to be loved.

(ii) Love means appetite. Here is no concern, only need for satisfaction.

(iii) Love means affectionate contact with the mother.

(iv) Love means integration (on the part of the infant) of the object of instinctual experience with the whole mother of affectionate contact; giving becomes related to taking, etc.

(v) Love means staking a claim on the mother, being greedy under compulsion, forcing the mother to make up for the (inevitable) deprivations for which she is responsible.

(vi) Love means caring for the mother (or substitute object) as the mother cared for the infant – a preview of an adult attitude of responsibility.

CONCLUSION

These developments (and many others) can be seen in the first year, though of course nothing is established at the first birthday, and almost all can be lost by a breakdown of environmental provision after that date, or even through anxieties that are inherent in emotional maturation.

The paediatrician may well feel appalled when he attempts to master the psychology of the infant, briefly sketched here. Nevertheless he need not despair, for he can usually leave it all to the infant, the mother, and the father. But if he must interfere with the infant-mother relationship let him at least know what he is doing, and let him avoid all interference that is avoidable.

2

The Relationship of a Mother to
her Baby at the Beginning

THE NURSING COUPLE

In an examination of the relationship that exists between a mother and an infant it is necessary to separate out that which belongs to the mother and that which is starting to develop in the infant. Two distinct kinds of identification are involved, the mother's identification with her infant, and the infant's state of identification with the mother. The mother brings to the situation a developed capacity, whereas the infant is in this state because this is the way things begin.

We notice in the expectant mother an increasing identification with the infant. The infant links up with the idea of an 'internal object' in the mother, an object imagined to be set up inside and maintained there in spite of all the persecutory elements that also have place there. The baby has other meanings for the mother in the unconscious fantasy, but the predominant feature may be a willingness as well as an ability on the part of the mother to drain interest from her own self on to the baby. I have referred to this aspect of a mother's attitude as 'primary maternal preoccupation'.

In my view this is the thing that gives the mother her special ability to do the right thing. She knows what the baby could be feeling like. No one else knows. Doctors and nurses may know a lot about psychology, and of course they know all about body health and disease. But they do not know what a baby feels like from minute to minute because they are outside this area of experience.

There are two kinds of maternal disorder that affect this issue. At one extreme is the mother whose self-interests are too compulsive to be abandoned, so that she fails to plunge into this extraordinary condition which is almost like an illness, though it is very much a sign of health. At the other extreme is the mother who tends to be preoccupied in any case, and the baby now becomes her *pathological* preoccupation. This mother may have a special capacity for lending her own self to her infant, but what happens at the end? It is part of the normal process that the mother recovers her self-interest, and does so at the rate at which her infant can allow her to do so. The pathologically preoccu-

15

pied mother not only goes on being identified with her baby too long, but also she changes suddenly from preoccupation with the infant to her former preoccupation.

The normal mother's recovery from her preoccupation with her infant provides a kind of weaning. The first kind of ill mother cannot wean her infant because her infant has never had ner, and so weaning has no meaning; the other kind of ill mother cannot wean, or she tends to wean suddenly, and without regard for the gradually developing need of the infant to be weaned.

We can find parallels to all these things if we look at our own therapeutic work with children. The children in our care, in so far as they have a need for therapy, are going through phases in which they go back and experience again (or experience for the first time with us) the early relationships which were not satisfactory in their past history. We are able to identify with them as the mother identifies herself with her infant, temporarily but fully.

We are on safe ground when thinking in terms of this sort of thing that happens to parents, whereas when thinking of *a maternal instinct* we get bogged down in theory, and we get lost in a mix-up of human beings and animals. Most animals do in fact manage this early mothering pretty well, and at the early stages of the evolutionary process reflexes and simple instinctual responses sufficed. But somehow or other human mothers and babies have human qualities and these must be respected. They also have reflexes and crude instincts, but we cannot satisfactorily describe human beings in terms of that which they share with animals.

It is important, although perhaps obvious, that when the mother is in the state that I have described she is highly vulnerable. This is not always noticed, because of the fact that there is usually some sort of provision around the mother, perhaps organized by her man. These secondary phenomena can arrange themselves naturally around a pregnancy just like the mother's special state around the infant. It is when there is a breakdown of the natural protective forces that one notices how vulnerable the mother is. Here we are on to a big subject which joins up with that of the mental disorders called puerperal, to which women are liable. Not only is the development of primary maternal preoccupation difficult for some women to attain, but also the return from it to a normal attitude to life and to the self may produce clinical illness. Such illness can be brought about to some extent by failure of the protective covering, failure of that which enables the mother to be in-turned and oblivious of external danger while she is preoccupied maternally.

THE INFANT'S IDENTIFICATION WITH THE MOTHER

In examining the infant's state of identification I am concerned with the infant at full term, with the new-born infant, and with the infant a few weeks or months old. An infant that is six months old is passing right out of the stage I am now considering.

The problem is so delicate and complex that we cannot hope to get any-where in our thinking unless we assume that the infant under consideration has a good-enough mother. Only if there is a good-enough mother does the infant start on a process of development that is personal and real. If the mothering is not good enough then the infant becomes a collection of reactions to impingement, and the true self of the infant fails to form or becomes hidden behind a false self which complies with and generally wards off the world's knocks.

We will ignore this complication, and look at the infant that has a good-enough mother and that does really start. Of this infant I would say: the ego is both weak and strong. All depends on the capacity of the mother to give ego support. The mother's ego is attuned to the ego of the infant, and she can give support only if she is able to orientate to her infant in the way that I have partially described.

When there is a mother-infant couple in good working order the infant's ego is very strong indeed, because the infant ego is supported in all respects. The infant's reinforced and therefore strong ego is able very early to organize defences, and to develop patterns that are personal and that are strongly coloured by hereidtary tendencies.

This description of the ego that is both weak and strong applies also to the state of affairs when a patient (child or adult) is regressed and dependent in the therapeutic situation. My purpose, however, is to describe the infant. It is this infant whose ego is strong *because of the mother's ego support* that early becomes himself or herself, really and truly. Where the mother's ego support is absent, or weak, or patchy, the infant cannot develop along personal lines, and development is then related, as I have said, more to a succession of reactions to environmental failure than to the internal urges and genetic factors. It is the well-cared-for babies who quickly establish themselves as persons, each different from any other infant that ever was, whereas the babies who receive inadequate or pathological ego support tend to be alike in patterns of behaviour (restless, suspicious, apathetic, inhibited, compliant). In the therapeutic child-care situation one is often rewarded by the emergence of a child who is for the first time an individual.

This bit of theory is needed if one is to reach to the place where infants live – a queer place – where *nothing has yet been separated out as not-me*, so there is *not yet a* ME. Here identification is what the infant *starts with*. It is not that the infant identifies himself or herself with the mother, but rather that no mother, no object external to the self, is known; and even this state-ment is wrong because there is not yet a self. It could be said that the self of the infant at this very early stage is only potential. In a *return* to this state an individual becomes merged in with the mother's self. The infant self has not yet formed and so cannot be said to be merged, but memories and expectations can now start to accumulate and to form. We must remember that these things occur only when the infant's ego is strong because reinforced.

When we consider this state of the infant we have to go one stage further back than we usually do. For instance, we know about disintegration, and this leads easily to the idea of integration. But in this context we need a word like *unintegration*, in order to convey our meaning. Similarly we know about depersonalization, and this leads easily to the idea that there is a process of becoming a person, a process of establishing unity or liaison between the body or body functions and the psyche (whatever that exactly means). But in considering early growth we need to think of the infant as not yet having begun to have a problem here, for at our stage the psyche is only beginning to elaborate itself around body functioning.

Again, we know about object relationships, and from here we easily get to the idea of a process of establishing a capacity for relating to objects. But it is necessary to think of a state of affairs before the concept of an object has meaning to the infant, although the infant is experiencing satisfaction in relating to something that we see to be an object, or what we may call a part-object.

These very primitive matters get started up when the mother, identifying with her infant, is able and willing to give support just when it is needed.

THE MATERNAL FUNCTION

On the basis of these considerations it is possible to categorize the function of the good-enough mother in the early stages. These can be boiled down to:

  (i) Holding
 (ii) Handling
(iii) Object-presenting.

(i) Holding is very much related to the mother's capacity to identify with her infant. Satisfactory holding is a basic ration of care, only experienced in the reactions to faulty holding. Faulty holding produces extreme distress in the infant, giving a basis for:

the sense of going to pieces,
the sense of falling for ever,
the feeling that external reality cannot be used for reassurance,
and other anxieties that are usually described as 'psychotic'.

(ii) Handling facilitates the formation of a psychosomatic partnership in the

18

infant. This contributes to the sense of 'real', as opposed to 'unreal'. Faulty handling militates against the development of muscle tone, and that which is called 'coordination', and against the capacity of the infant to enjoy the experience of body functioning, and of BEING.

(iii) Object-presenting or *realizing* (that is, making real the infant's creative impulse) initiates the infant's capacity to relate to objects. Faulty object presenting further blocks the way for the development of the infant's capacity to feel real in relating to the actual world of objects and phenomena.

Briefly, development is a matter of the inheritance of a *maturational process*, and of the accumulation of living experiences; this development does not occur, however, except in a *facilitating environment*. The facilitating environment is first absolutely and then relatively important, and the course of development can be described in terms of absolute dependence, relative dependence, and towards independence.

SUMMARY

Here then I have attempted to make a statement of the infant's end of the mother-infant coupling. What we find is not strictly speaking identification at all. It is something that is unorganized becoming organized under highly specialized conditions, and separating out gradually from the facilitating matrix. This is what forms in the womb, and it is this which gradually evolves into a human being. But this is not something that can take place in a test-tube, even a large one. We witness, even if we do not see, the evolution of the immature nursing-couple experience, a mother-infant partnership in which the mother by one kind of identification meets the infant's original state of undifferentiation. Without the special state of the mother that I have referred to there can be no true emergence of the infant from the original state. The best that can happen then is the development of a false self hiding what vestige there may be of a true self.

In our *therapeutic* work over and over again we become involved with a patient; we pass through a phase in which we are vulnerable (as the mother is) because of our involvement; we are identified with the child who is temporarily dependent on us to an alarming degree; we watch the shedding of the child's false self or false selves; we see the new beginning of a true self, a true self with an ego that is strong because like the mother with her infant we have been able to give ego support. If all goes well, we may find that a child has emerged, a child whose ego can organize its own defences against the anxieties that belong to id impulse and experience. A 'new' being is born, because of what we do, a real human being capable of having an independent life. My thesis is that what we do in therapy is to attempt to imitate the natural process that characterizes the behaviour of any mother of her own infant. If I am right, it is the mother-infant couple that can teach us the basic principles on which we may base our therapeutic work, when we are treating children whose early mothering was 'not good enough', or was interrupted.

3

Growth and Development
in Immaturity

The reader should know that I am a product of the Freudian or psycho-analytic school. This does not mean that I take for granted everything Freud said or wrote, and in any case that would be absurd since Freud was developing, that is to say changing, his views (in an orderly manner, like any other scientific worker) all along the line right up to his death in 1939.

As a matter of fact, there are some things that Freud came to believe which seem to me and to many other analysts to be actually wrong, but it simply does not matter. The point is that Freud started off a scientific approach to the problem of human development; he broke through the reluctance to speak openly of sex and especially of infant and child sexuality, and he accepted the instincts as basic and worthy of study; he gave us a method for use and for development which we could learn, and whereby we could check the observations of others and contribute our own; he demonstrated the repressed unconscious and the operation of unconscious conflict; he insisted on the full recognition of psychic reality (what is real to the individual apart from what is actual); he boldly attempted to formulate theories of the mental processes, some of which have already become generally accepted.

Arising out of all this is something that is relevant here. Each individual starts and develops and becomes mature; there is no adult maturity apart from the previous development. This development is extremely complex, and it is continuous from birth or earlier right up to and through adulthood to old age. We cannot afford to leave anything out, not even the happenings of infancy, not even those of very early infancy.

Here we should pause to think about our aims in our work. We are concerned with the provision of the environment that is appropriate to the age of the infant, toddler, or child; the environment that will enable each individual gradually and in his own way to become a person who can take a place in the community without losing his or her own individuality. We do not want the children in our care to become persons who belong to an extreme category: either those who are indeed community-minded, but whose private lives are unsatisfactory so that they do not have a sense of the self going on; or those who maintain their own personal satisfactions only by neglecting their relation

21

to society, or perhaps by being antisocial or insane. For we know that people who have to be classed in these two extremes are unhappy; they are suffering. Some of them achieve personal expression only in the act of suicide. Someone has failed them or something has gone wrong environmentally at one or more of the earlier stages, and at a late date it is hard to put things right.

But to return to the subject of young children. When we give children the right kind of good time there is really an aim in it all, namely, to make possible each child's ultimate growth to the adult state which collectively is called democracy. We know, however, how important it is not to put children in a position that is too advanced for them. Moreover, we know how futile it is to 'teach' democracy as distinct from enabling individuals to grow up, to mature, to become the stuff democracy is made of.[1]

I would mention here some of the early equivalents of what may later become, given favourable circumstances, the material for democracy. I leave out of account the management of older children, allowing them to take part in clubs and various institutions appropriate to their age. At an earlier stage, however, there is the germ of this, surely, in allowing children to take over community functions *temporarily*. We would not expect cubs or brownies to run their own groups, but we would expect there to be *moments* in which a cub or a brownie might wish to play at being in charge. And play is serious as well as enjoyable.

Sometimes an elder sister has to be a mother, with very great responsibilities, at an early age, and we can see how this task, well performed, drains away the girl's spontaneity and sense of her own self's rights; these things cannot be avoided. But ordinarily any child will like to be the responsible person *for limited periods of time*. This works best when it is the child's idea and not an idea imposed by ourselves. But gradually children become able to identify with us and so to accept our sensible impositions without too great a loss of their sense of self and the self's rights.

Is there not something of this in the evolution of children's drawings? First comes messing and then scribbling. Then the child means things in the scribbling, but we would not know what unless we were informed. The child sees anything and everything in the marks made. Perhaps the line goes over the edge and that is equivalent to bed-wetting, or to some actual messing (an upset teacup) that was nice for the child even if inconvenient for the adult. Then perhaps a rough circle turns up and the child says 'duck'. Now the child has begun to express more than the fun of instinctual experience. There is a new gain here, and for this the child is willing to forgo some of the pleasure of a more direct instinctual kind. Soon, all too soon, the child is putting legs and arms on the circle and eyes in the inside, and we say 'Humpty-Dumpty'.

[1] This theme is developed in the final section, 'Some thoughts on the meaning of the word democracy' (p. 155 below)

We all laugh, and already direct expression is a long way away and drawing has started. But once more there is a gain because of the constructive nature of what is being done, which is recognized by someone near and dear to the child, and also because a new form of communication has been discovered which is better than speech. In no time the child is drawing pictures. The size and shape of the page determine the placing of the objects depicted. There comes a balance of objects and of movements, and a subtle interrelationship of all the relative proportions. The child is now an artist for a brief spell. More important, the child has shown a developing capacity to retain spontaneity while respecting form and all the other controls. This is the democratic idea in miniature. It is but weakly established as yet because it depends on some person who is in relation to the child that is drawing. Later, this very personal tie is broken, and must be broken and diffused, and before the child is either eventually an artist, or more likely an ordinary citizen, he or she has to be able to supply *from within* this person in relation to whom, externally, the early artistry was so richly shown.

All this leads us back and back. In terms of environment, this earlier and earlier means more and more personal, and it means that the person who is personal with the child needs to be more and more reliable.

Gradually as we go still further back the person has to be able to be even more than reliable from the child's point of view. We know that with small children it is only love of the particular child that enables the person to be reliable enough. We love a child and maintain an uninterrupted relationship and half the battle is won. But let us go yet further back. Now even stronger words have to be used. I think that over the relatively short period of the first months the word 'devotion' takes us exactly where we need to go. I am not using words like 'clever', 'learned', 'well taught', although I do not despise them. Only a devoted mother (or mother-surrogate) can follow an infant's needs. As I see it, the infant at the start needs a degree of *active adaptation to needs* which cannot be provided unless a devoted person is doing everything. It is obvious that it is the infant's own mother to whom such devotion comes naturally, and even if it can be proved that infants do not know their mothers till they are some months old I still think we must assume that the mother knows her infant.

EDUCATION OF PARENTS

I may be criticized here. The reader may say: 'But you are taking it for granted that mothers are normal and you are forgetting that many are neurotic and some are near-insane.' 'Many are getting a poor deal themselves, and they pass on their sexual frustrations to their infants by being irritable or in more direct ways.' 'It is absurd to talk about mothers acting naturally, or nurses or teachers or anyone. *They have all got to be taught.*'

My answer is not to disagree absolutely; but I would say that when people who care for infants and children are neurotic or near-insane (and many are), they cannot be taught. Our hope lies in those who are more or less normal. In our clinics we have to deal with the abnormalities, and we orientate towards abnormality. But in managing ordinary mothers and infants, and in teaching infants and young children, *we must resolutely keep orientated towards the normal or healthy.* And healthy mothers have much to teach us.

Are we quite sure that the doctors and nurses who so skilfully care for mothers in antenatal clinics, in maternity wards, and in welfare clinics really allow the ordinary healthy mother to function? Things have improved very much in the last few years. Now it is not so rare to see maternity hospitals with the babies in baskets beside their mothers. I need not draw a picture of the horrid alternative which is all too well known, of the infant in the infant ward, brought in at feed-time and pushed up against the breast of the bewildered and even frightened mother. Also, largely because of the work of Bowlby and Robertson,[1] there is now a greater tendency to allow parents to keep in touch with their infants and small children who unfortunately need to have a spell in hospital.

The fact is that doctors and nurses have to recognize that they are experts in one direction only. In regard to such a thing as the beginning of an emotional relationship between the mother and the baby (of which the establishment of breast-feeding is a part), the ordinary mother is not only the expert; she is actually the only one who can know how to act for that particular baby. There is a reason. It is because of her *devotion*, which is the only motivation that works.

When we attempt to carry over this consideration to such a complex thing as the nursery school, we can say, greatly simplifying, that in any nursery school there must be two kinds of children – and the same is true of all schools. There are those children whose parents have managed well and are managing well. These children will be the rewarding children, able to show and cope with all kinds of feelings. Then there are the children whose parents have not succeeded, and we must remember that the failure may not be their fault at all. It may be a doctor's fault, or a nurses's fault; or it may have come about through the operation of chance – for instance, a bad attack of whooping cough; or perhaps willing helpers got in the way. These children need, at nursery-school age, the active adaptation to needs that belongs truly to the

[1] John Bowlby, *Maternal Care and Mental Health* (London: HMSO, 1951); abridged version, edited by Margery Fry, *Child Care and the Growth of Love* (Harmondsworth: Penguin Books, 1953). James Robertson, *Young Children in Hospital* (London: Tavistock Publications, 1958). See also two films by James Robertson, *A Two-year-old goes to Hospital* and *Going to Hospital with Mother* (Tavistock Child Development Research Unit, 2 Beaumont Street, London, W1).

earliest weeks and months. They may need it from persons who are not their actual parents. Active adaptation coming too late is called 'spoiling', and those who spoil a child are criticized. Moreover, since this active adaptation to needs comes too late the children cannot make proper use of it, or else they need it to a very great degree and over a long period. Thus the person who is able to supply it may find himself in a very difficult situation because the child may develop a dependence on him that he dare not break.

The thing is that all schools should be in triplicate:

(a) For the children of the first class that I have described, who can enrich themselves from what is offered to them and can contribute and gain by contributing.

(b) For the children who need from the teachers what home has failed to supply, that is psychotherapy rather than teaching.

(c) For the intermediates.

THE LIVING CHILD

I would like now to turn this subject inside out, and to describe the infant and the child in terms of the development of the living child.

First I would simplify matters by separating out the *excited state* from the *unexcited state*. The *excited state* obviously implies the operation of instincts. As we know, every bodily functioning has its imaginative elaboration, and so the conflicts that develop in respect of ideas involve inhibitions and muddles in bodily happening; growth here implies not only going from stage to stage because of increasing age, but also the negotiation of each state as it is reached, without too much loss of the instinctual roots of feeling. It is just in these early stages of instinct development, however, that the serious repressions start that cripple the lives of many individuals. How necessary then, for the toddler, are a stability and a continuity of environment, in both its physical and its emotional aspects!

Although it is just here that the main forces of dynamic psychology are to be found I feel that I need not reiterate these points. Freud's work, which has chiefly dealt with these vital phenomena, is now fairly widely known, especially by those who study the psychology of children.

The various instinctual drives that almost rend the infant by their strength develop according to a natural progression. At first, naturally, it is the mouth and the whole intake mechanisms, including the grasping of the hands, that form the basis for the fantasy that exists at the height of excitement. Later the excretory phenomena provide material for excited fantasy, and what goes on inside too. In the course of time a genital type of excitement turns up and can be said to dominate the life of the little boy or girl in the two to five age group.

The natural progression of these various types of excited ideas and of excitement organizations is not usually clear and simple because at all stages conflicts arise, and the very best management cannot alter this fact. Good management is more of the nature of providing consistent conditions in which each infant can work out what is specific to that infant.

Naturally, the ideas that belong to excited times form the basis for play and for dreams. In play there is excitement of a special kind, and play is spoiled when direct instinctual need comes to the fore. Only gradually do infants come to the management of these matters. Indeed, all adults know how the pleasures of life can be spoiled by the intrusion of bodily excitement, and part of the technique of living is to find ways of avoiding bodily excitements that cannot come soon to climax. Naturally this is easier for those whose instinctual life is satisfactory than for those who cannot avoid having to tolerate a high degree of frustration in sexual relationships.

Fortunately, while children are gradually finding out these difficult things they can reach satisfactory climaxes in all sorts of ways that are characteristic for children. Food can do a lot, for instance. Also sleep resolves a great deal. Defecation and urination can be extremely satisfactory experiences, and so can a good fight or being smacked. Nevertheless, in every childhood there are manifold symptoms that quite clearly reflect the condition known as 'being all dressed up and nowhere to go'; excited, without the capacity for reaching a climax (bilious attacks, etc.). These things are not necessarily abnormal.

Many people now know a great deal about all these things, but they may not know about some of the more *indirect* results of instinctual experience. I refer now to the way the richness of the personality builds up through satisfactory and unsatisfactory experiences.

It is helpful to postulate here an early *ruthless* stage in order to draw attention to the fact that at first the excited and highly destructive ideas that go with instinctual experience are directed at the mother's breast without guilt. In health, however, the infant soon comes to put two and two together and to know that what is in fantasy so ruthlessly attacked is the same as that which is loved and needed. The ruthless stage gives way to a stage of *concern*.

The infant now has to deal with two sets of phenomena after a satisfactory excited experience. A good thing has been attacked and hurt and spoiled, and moreover the infant is richer for the experience; something good has been built up inside The infant has to be able to stand feeling guilt. In the course of time a way out of the trouble appears, because the infant is able to find *ways of making reparation*, of mending, of giving in return, of putting back what has (in fantasy) been stolen. (Readers will recognize Melanie Klein in all this.)

We can see, then, that there is a specific need here which the environment

26

must supply if the infant is to come through and grow (technically: to reach the 'depressive position' in emotional development). The infant has to be able to tolerate feeling guilt, and to alter this state of affairs by making reparation. If this is to happen, the mother (or someone in her place) has to stay there, alive and alert, over the guilt period. To put it crudely: an infant in an institution might be beautifully cared for by several nurses, but what if the guilt belonging to the morning's experiences comes up for repair in the evening when another nurse is there, and so the reparation misses fire. The mother caring for her own infant is more or less always there and recognizes the spontaneous constructive and reparative impulses. She can wait for them and she recognizes them when they come.

When all goes well it is not guilt that is experienced, but a sense of being responsible develops. The sense of guilt remains latent, to appear when reparation fails relative to destruction.

Much more could be said about all this guilt and reparation, and about the infant's anxieties in respect of the riches that are storing up inside. If we looked we should find frightening things in there too, inside the baby, arising out of the baby's angry impulses. But I now want to leave consideration of the excited states and of the consequences of excited experiences in order to get on to something else. Let me say in passing that difficulties in this field, associated with the repression of painful conflicts, lead on to the various neurotic manifestations and to mood disorders. If we study the material of the unexcited states, however, we shall be nearer to a study of psychosis. Disorders of what I describe under the heading of unexcited states will be found to be psychotic rather than neurotic in quality, the stuff insanity is made of. However, I am not dealing with disorders; instead I am briefly describing the tasks which the infant has to perform in making an ordinary healthy development.

DEVELOPMENT APART FROM EXCITEMENTS

If we turn, then, rather artificially, to the *unexcited state*, what do we find? For one thing we find we are studying the ego in the self's journey towards autonomy. We are studying, for instance, the development in the infant of a sense of unity of personality, a capacity to feel (at any rate at times) *integrated*. Gradually, too, the infant begins to feel to be a dweller in what we so easily see as that infant's own body. All these things take time, and are greatly helped by sensible and consistent management of the body, bathing, exercising, and so on.

Then there is also the development of a capacity to *relate to* external reality. This task which every infant must achieve is complex and difficult, and very definitely needs the attention that a devoted mother is qualified to give. The *objectively* perceived world is *never* the same as what is conceived of, what is seen *subjectively*. This is a big trouble with all human beings, but by actively adapting at the start a mother superimposes external reality on what the infant conceives of; she does this well enough, and often enough, so that the infant becomes contented to leave this problem to be taken up later as part of the game called philosophy.

One more thing: if the environment behaves well, the infant has a chance to maintain a sense of *continuity of being*; perhaps this may go right back to the first stirrings in the womb. When this exists the individual has a stability that can be gained in no other way.

If external reality has been introduced to the infant in small doses, accurately graded to the infant's or child's understanding, the child may grow up to be capable of making a scientific approach to phenomena, and may even perhaps carry a scientific method into the study of human affairs. If this happens, and if it is successful, then there is something owing to the devoted mother who laid the foundations, and then to both the fond parents, and then to a succession of minders and teachers, any of whom could have caused a muddle and could have made difficult the child's ultimate attainment of a scientific attitude. Most of us, alas, have to put at least some of human nature outside the realm of scientific inquiry.

SCIENCE AND HUMAN NATURE

The main burden of this communication is that if what is true and good and natural in human nature and in the management of growing human beings is to be saved from being squashed out by science, it can only come about by an extension of scientific inquiry into the whole field of human nature. I think we are all travelling towards the same thing. To restate it: we want to make it possible for each individual to find and establish his or her own identity in such a solid way that eventually, in the course of time, and in that individual's own manner, there will be attained a capacity to become a member of society – an active, creative member, without loss of personal spontaneity and without loss of that sense of freedom which comes, in health, from within.

CLINICAL CODA

It may well be that the reader is left with a feeling of bewilderment. There is so much for the infant to go through, and the responsibility of the mothers and fathers and nurses and teachers who provide the environment suitable for the various stages is so great, how shall we ever manage? But it must be remembered that whenever we pause in our work and attempt to make some assessment of our aims, as we have done now, we have an artificial situation.

And so, let us return to the real thing, and conclude with the picture of a rather young baby boy. (It could as well be a girl.)

This baby has been through all the usual things, fist-sucking, finger-sucking, scratching the skin of his belly, pulling at his navel and his penis, and plucking at the wool of the cover. He is about eight months old and he has not yet quite taken up with the usual run of teddies and dolls. But he has found some soft object. He has adopted this object. Eventually there will be a special name for it. It will remain a necesssary thing in the child's life for some years, and in the end will simply fade away like the old soldier. This object is halfway between everything. *We* know that it came from an aunt. From the infant's point of view however it is the perfect compromise. It is neither part of the self nor part of the world. Yet it is both. It was conceived of by the infant and yet he could not have produced it, it just came. Its coming showed him what to conceive of. It is at one and the same time subjective and objective. It is at the border between inside and outside. It is both dream and real.

We leave this baby with this object. In his relationship with it he is at peace, in the celtic twilight between a personal or psychic reality and reality that is actual and shared.

4

On Security

Whenever an attempt is made to state the basic needs of infants and children, we hear the words 'what children need is security'. Sometimes we may feel this is sensible and at other times we may feel doubtful. It may be asked, what does the word 'security' mean? Certainly parents who are over-protective cause distress in their children, just as parents who cannot be reliable make their children muddled and frightened. Evidently, then, it is possible for parents to give too much security, and yet we know that children do need to feel secure. How can we sort this out?

Parents who can manage to keep a home together do in fact provide something that is immensely important to their children, and naturally when a home breaks up there are casualties among the children. But if we are just simply told that children need security, we feel that something must be missing from this statement. Children find in security a sort of challenge, a challenge to them to prove that they can break out. The extreme of the idea that security is good would be that a prison is a happy place to grow up in. This would be absurd. Of course there can be freedom of the spirit anywhere, even in a prison. The poet Lovelace wrote:

> *Stone walls do not a prison make,*
> *Nor iron bars a cage,*

implying that there is more to be thought of than the actual fact of being held fast. But people must live freely in order to live imaginatively. Freedom is an essential element, something that brings out the best in people. Nevertheless, we have to admit that there are some who cannot live in freedom because they fear both themselves and the world.

To sort out these ideas, I think we must consider the developing infant, the child, the adolescent, the adult, and trace the evolution, not only of individual persons, but also of what they need from the environment as they evolve. Certainly it is a sign of healthy growth when children begin to be able to enjoy the freedom that can increasingly be given to them. What are we aiming at in bringing up children? We hope that each child will gradually acquire a sense of security. There must build up inside each child a belief in something not only something that is good but also something that is reliable and

30

durable, or that recovers after having been hurt or allowed to perish. The question is, how does this building-up of a sense of security take place? What leads to this satisfactory state of affairs in which the child has confidence in the people around and in things? What brings out the quality we call self-confidence? Is the important thing an innate or personal factor, or is it moral teaching? Must there be an example that is to be copied? Is an external environmental provision necessary to produce the desired effect?

We could review the stages of emotional development through which every child must pass in order to become a healthy and eventually an adult person. In the course of this review we could talk of the innate processes of growth in the individual and the way (necessarily very complex) in which human beings become persons in their own right. Here, however, I want to refer to the environmental provision, the part we play and the part that society plays in relation to us. It is the surroundings that make it possible for each child to grow, and without adequate environmental reliability the personal growth of a child cannot take place, or such growth must be distorted. Furthermore, as no two children are exactly alike we are required to adapt specifically to each child's needs. This means that whoever is caring for a child must know that child and must work on the basis of a personal living relationship with that child, not on the basis of something learnt and applied mechanically. Being reliably present and consistently ourselves we provide a stability which is not rigid, but alive and human, and this makes the infant feel secure. It is this in relation to which the infant can grow, and which the infant can absorb and copy.

When we offer security we do two things at once. On the one hand, because of our help the child is safe from the unexpected, from innumerable unwelcome intrusions, and from a world that is not yet known or understood. And also, on the other hand, the child is protected by us from his or her own impulses and from the effects that these impulses might produce. It is hardly necessary to say that very young infants need care absolutely and cannot get on on their own. They need to be held, to be moved, to be cleaned up, to be fed, to be kept at the right temperature, and to be protected from draughts and bangs. They need their impulses to be met and they need us to make sense of their spontaneity. There is not much difficulty at this early stage because in most cases the infant has a mother, and the mother for a time concerns herself almost entirely with her infant's needs. At this stage the infant is secure. When a mother succeeds in this thing that she does at the beginning, the result may be a child whose difficulties really do belong, not to the impingements of the world, but to life and to the conflict that goes with live feelings. In the most satisfactory circumstances, then, in the security of infant care that is good enough, the infant starts living a personal and individual life.

Very soon infants begin to be able to defend themselves against insecurity, but in the first weeks and months they are but feebly established as persons and so, if unsupported, they become distorted in their development when untoward things happen. The infant that has known security at this early stage begins to carry around an expectation that he or she won't be 'let down'. Frustrations—well, yes, these are inevitable; but being let down—well, no!

The question we are concerned with here is, what happens when a sense of security becomes established in the child? I want to say this. There then follows one long struggle *against* security, that is to say security that is provided in the environment. The mother, after the initial period of protection, gradually lets the world in, and the individual small child now pounces on every new opportunity for free expression and for impulsive action. This war against security and against controls continues throughout childhood; yet the controls go on being necessary. The parents continue to be ready with a disciplinary framework, with the stone walls and iron bars, but in so far as they know what each child is like, and in so far as they are concerned with the evolution of their children as persons, they welcome the children's defiance. They continue to function as custodians of the peace but they expect lawlessness and even revolution. Fortunately, in most cases relief is obtained both for the children and for the parents through the life of imagination and play, and through cultural experiences. In time and in health children become able to retain a sense of security in the face of manifest insecurity, as for instance when a parent is ill or dies, or when someone misbehaves, or when a home for some reason or other breaks up.

THE NEED TO TEST SECURITY MEASURES

Children need to go on finding out whether they can still rely on their parents, and this testing may continue till the children are themselves ready to provide secure conditions for their own children, and after. Adolescents quite characteristically make tests of all security measures and of all rules and regulations and disciplines. So it usually happens that children do accept security as a basic assumption. They believe in good early mothering and fathering because they have had these. They carry with them a sense of security and this is constantly being reinforced by their tests of their parents and family, of their schoolteachers and friends, and of all sorts of people they meet. Having found the locks and bolts securely fastened, they proceed to unlock them and to break them open; they burst out. And again and again they burst out. Or else they curl up in bed and play blue jazz records and feel futile.

Why do adolescents especially make such tests? It seems to be mainly because they are meeting frighteningly new and strong feelings in themselves, and they wish to know that the external controls are still there. But at the same time they must prove that they can break through these controls and establish themselves as themselves. Healthy children do need people to go on being in control, but the disciplines must be provided by persons who can be loved and hated, defied and depended on; mechanical controls are of no use, nor can fear be a good motive for compliance. It is always a living relationship between persons that gives the elbow room which is necessary for true growth. True growth gradually, and in the course of time, carries the child or adolescent on to an adult sense of responsibility, especially responsibility for the provision of secure conditions for the small children of a new generation.

We can see all this going on in the work of creative artists of all kinds. They do something very valuable for us, because they are constantly creating new forms and breaking through these forms only to create new ones. Artists enable us to keep alive, when the experiences of real life often threaten to destroy our sense of being alive and real in a living way. Artists best of all people remind us that the struggle between our impulses and the sense of security (both of which are vital to us) is an eternal struggle and one that goes on inside each one of us as long as our life lasts.

In health, then, children develop enough belief in themselves and in other people to hate external controls of all kinds; controls have changed over into self-control. In self-control the conflict *has been worked through within the person* in advance. So I see it this way: good conditions in the early stages lead to a sense of security, and a sense of security leads on to self-control, and when self-control is a fact, then security that is imposed is an insult.

5

The Five-Year-Old

In a court of law a learned judge is reported to have said, with reference to the case of a child of nearly five whose parents had split up: 'Children of that age are notoriously resilient.' I have no wish to criticize the judgement given in this case, but it is open to us to discuss the question: Are children of five years notoriously resilient? Resilience, it would seem to me, comes only with growth and maturity, and we may hold the view that there is no time in the development of a child at which it could be said that the child is resilient. Resilience would imply that we could expect compliance on the part of the child without danger to the growth of the child's personality and to the establishment of the child's character.

It might indeed be argued that there are some special features of this five-year-old stage which would make us particularly careful *not* to relax our watch on environmental reliability. It is these special features that I wish to consider here.

Parents watch their children grow, and they are astonished. It is all so slow, and yet at the same time it all happens in a flash. That is the funny thing about it. A few weeks ago they had a baby; and then he was a toddler; and today he is five, and tomorrow he will be at school – or she – whichever applies. And in a few weeks he will practically have started going to work.

There is a contradiction here which is interesting. The time passed both slowly and quickly. Or, to put it another way, when the parents were feeling things from the point of view of the child, time practically stood still. Or it started off still, and only gradually began to move. The idea of eternity comes from the memory traces in each one of us of our infancy before time started. But when we jump across to having our own grown-up experiences, we realize that five years are almost nothing.

This has a curious effect on the relationship between what the parents remember and what the child remembers. They themselves remember clearly what happened a month ago, and now suddenly they find that their five-year-old is not remembering his aunt's visit or the arrival of the new puppy. He remembers some things, even early things, especially if these have been talked about, and he uses the family saga which he learns almost as if it were about someone else, or as if it referred to characters in a book. He has become more aware of himself and of the present time, and along with this he has come to forget. He now has a past, and in his mind a hint of half-forgotten things. His teddy bear is at the back of the bottom drawer, and he has forgotten how important it once was, except when he suddenly feels a need for it again.

We could say that he is emerging from an enclosure: the walls of the enclosure began to have gaps, and the fences became uneven in thickness; and lo and behold, the child is outside. It is not easy for him to get back inside again or to feel that he is back inside, unless he is tired or ill, when the enclosure is re-assembled for his benefit.

The enclosure was provided by his mother and his father, by his family, by the house and the courtyard, and by the familiar sights and noises and smells. It also belongs to his own stage of immaturity, to his reliance on his parents' reliability, and to the subjective nature of the infant world. This enclosure was a natural development from the mother's arms that were put round him when he was an infant. She adapted in an intimate way to her infant's needs, and then she gradually de-adapted, according to the rate at which he became able to enjoy meeting the unexpected and the new. And so, since children are not really very like each other, the mother finds that she has made an enclosure in which each child lives, one for each child; and it is out of this enclosure that her son or daughter now emerges – ready for a different kind of group, a new kind of enclosure, at least for a few hours a day. In other words, the child will go to school.

Wordsworth referred to this change in his 'Ode on the Intimations of Immortality':

> Heaven lies about us in our infancy,
> Shades of the prison-house begin to close
> Upon the growing boy . . . .

Here surely, the poet felt the child's consciousness of the new enclosure, in contrast with the baby's unawareness of dependence.

Of course, the parents will already have started up the process by using a nursery school if a good one happens to be near where they live. In a good nursery school a small group of toddlers can be given opportunity for play, and can be provided with suitable toys, and perhaps a better floor than the one available at home; and someone is always present to supervise the child's first experiments in social life, such as bashing the next child on the head with a spade.

THE PRIMARY SCHOOL AT FIVE

But the nursery school is not much unlike home; it is still a specialized provision. The school we are now considering is different. The primary

35

school may be good or not so good, but it will not be adaptive like the nursery school, not specialized except perhaps at the very beginning. In other words the child will have to do the adapting, will have to fit in with what is expected of the pupils at the school. If he is ready for this, there is a great deal to be got out of the new experience.

The parents will have given a lot of thought to the management of this big change in their child's life. They will have talked about school, and the child has played at schools and has looked forward to the idea of experiencing an extension of the bit of teaching that his mother and father and others have already put in.

Difficulties do arise at this stage since environmental changes have to be fitted on to changes that are happening in the child because of growth. I have had quite a lot to do with difficulties of children at this age, and I would say this, that in the vast majority of cases of difficulty there is no deep-seated trouble at all, no real illness. The strain has to do with the need for one child to be quick, for another to be slow. A few months make a lot of difference. A child whose birthday is in November may be champing the bit waiting to be admitted, whereas a child whose birthday is in August may be packed off to school a month or two early. In any case, one child eagerly goes on to the deeper waters, whereas another tends to lie shivering on the brink and fears to launch away. And, by the way, some of the brave pushers-on suddenly shrink back after putting a toe in and go back inside their mother and refuse to re-emerge from the familiar enclosure for days or weeks or longer. The parents get to know what sort of a child they have, and they talk to the school-teachers, who are quite used to all this, and just wait, and play the fish on a long line. The thing is to understand that coming out of the enclosure is very exciting and very frightening; that, once out, it is awful for the child not being able to get back; and that life is a long series of coming out of enclosures and taking new risks and meeting new and exciting challenges.

Some children have personal difficulties that make them unable to take new steps, and the parents may need help if the passing of time does not bring cure, or if there are other indications of illness.

But it may be that there is something wrong with the mother, the perfectly good mother, when her child shrinks back. Some mothers operate in two layers. At one layer (shall I call it the top layer?) they want only one thing: they want their child to grow up, to get out of the enclosure, to go to school, to meet the world. At another layer, deeper, I suppose, and not really conscious, they cannot conceive of letting their child go. In this deeper layer where logic is not very important the mother cannot give up this most precious thing, her maternal function; she feels she is maternal more easily when her baby is dependent on her than when, by growth, he comes to enjoy being separate and independent and defiant.

36

The child senses this only too easily. Although happy at school, he comes panting home; he screams rather than go into the school door each morning. He is sorry for his mother because he knows that *she cannot stand losing him*, and that she has not got it in her to turn him out because of her nature. It is easier for the child if the mother can be glad to be rid of him, and glad to have him back.

A lot of people, including the best, are a bit depressed part of the time or almost all the time. They have a vague sense of guilt about something and they worry about their responsibilities. The liveliness of the child in the home has been a perpetural tonic. Always the child's noises, even his cries have been a sign of life, and have just given the right reassurance. For depressed people all the time feel that they may have let something die, something precious and essential. The time comes when their child is due to go to school and then the mother fears the emptiness of her home and of herself, the threat of a sense of internal personal failure which may drive her to find an alternative pre-occupation. When the child comes back from school, if a new preoccupation has come about, there will be no place for him, or he will have to fight his way back into the mother's centre. This fighting his way back becomes more important to him than school. The common result is that the child becomes a case of school refusal. All the time he is longing to be at school, and his mother longs for him to be just like other children.

Or it may be the father who complicates the issue in some such way, so that the child wants school but cannot get there or cannot stay there. And there are other reasons for school refusal, but these are not being enumerated here.

I knew a boy who at this stage developed a passion for joining things together with string. He was always tying the cushions to the mantlepiece and the chairs to the tables, so that it was precarious moving about in the house at all. He was very fond of his mother, but always uncertain of getting back to her centre because she quickly became depressed when he left her, and in no time she had replaced him with something else she was worried or doubtful about.[1]

Mothers who are a bit like this may perhaps be helped by understanding that these things often happen. Such a mother may be glad that her child is sensitive to his mother's and other people's feelings, but sorry that her unexpressed and even unconscious anxiety should make the child sorry for her. He is unable to get out of the enclosure.

The mother may have had an experience of this difficulty that the child is in at an earlier date. She may, for instance, have found it difficult to wean him. She may have come to recognize a pattern in his reluctance to take any new

[1] This case is referred to again in Section 9 below.

step or to explore the unknown. At each of these stages she was under threat of losing her child's dependence on her. She was in the process of acquiring a child with independence and a personal slant on life, and although she could see the advantages to be gained by this she could not get the necessary release of feeling. There is a very close relationship between this vaguely depressive state of mind – this preoccupation with undefined anxieties – and the capacity of a woman to give a child her full attention. It is not possible to consider the one without referring to the other. Most women live, I suppose, just on the borderline between concern and worry.

Mothers have all sorts of agonies to go through, and it is good when the babies and the children do not have to get caught up in them. They have plenty of agonies of their own. Actually they rather like having their own agonies, just as they like new skills, and a widening vision, and happiness.

What is this that Wordsworth calls 'The Shades of the Prison House'? In my language it is the changeover from the small child's living in a subjective world to the older child's living in a world of shared reality. The infant starts off in magical control of the environment – if he receives good-enough care – and creates the world anew, even his mother and the door-knob. By the age of five the child has become able to perceive his mother much as she is, to acknowledge a world of door-knobs and other objects that existed before his conception, and to recognize the fact of dependence just at the time when he is becoming truly independent. It is all a matter of timing, and most mothers manage it beautifully. Somehow or other people usually do.

FURTHER COMPLICATIONS

There are plenty of other ways in which life can affect children at this age. I mentioned the child's teddy bear. The child may well be addicted to some special object. This special object that was once a blanket or a napkin or the mother's scarf or a rag doll first became important for him or her before or after the first birthday, and especially at times of transition, as from waking to sleeping life. It is immensely important; it gets treated abominably; it even smells. It is lucky that the child uses this object and not the mother herself, or the lobe of her ear or her hair.

This object joins the child to external or shared reality. It is a part both of the child and of the mother. One child who has such an object may have no use for it during the day, but another will take it everywhere. At five the need for this thing may not have ceased, but many things can take its place – the child looks at comics, has a great variety of toys, both hard and soft, and there is the whole cultural life waiting to enrich the child's experience of living. But there may be trouble when the child goes to school, and the teacher will need to go slowly, and not ban this object absolutely from the classroom just at first. This problem nearly always resolves itself in a few weeks. I would say that the child is taking to school a bit of the relationship to his mother that dates right back to infantile dependence, and to early infancy, to the time when he was only beginning to recognize his mother and the world as separate from the self.

If the anxieties about going to school resolve themselves, then the boy will be able to give up taking this object along with him, and instead will have a truck or an engine in his pockets, as well as the string and the liquorice; and the girl will somehow manage by screwing up her handkerchief, or perhaps she will have a secret baby in a matchbox. In any case children can always suck their thumbs or bite their nails if hard put to it. As they gain confidence they usually give up these things. We learn to expect children to show anxiety about all moves away from being part and parcel of the mother and of home, moves towards citizenship of the wide, wide world. And anxiety may show as a return to infantile patterns which mercifully remain to provide reassurance. These patterns become a sort of built in psychotherapy which retains its effectiveness because the mother is alive and available, and because she is all the time providing a link between the present and the child's infancy experiences of which the infantile patterns are relics.

POSTSCRIPT

One other thing. Children tend to feel disloyal if they enjoy school and if they enjoy forgetting their mother for a few hours. So they vaguely feel anxious as they get near home, or they delay their return without knowing why. The mother who has reason to be angry with her child should not choose the moment of his or her return from school to express it. She, too, may be annoyed that she was forgotten, and must watch for her own reactions to the new developments. It would be better not to be cross about the ink on the tablecloth until she and her child have re-established contact. These things present no great difficulty if we know what is happening. Growing up is not all honey for the child, and for the mother it is often bitter aloes.

6

Integrative and Disruptive Factors
in Family Life *

It would be a truism to say that the family is an essential part of our civiliza-
tion. The way we arrange our families practically shows what our culture is
like, just as a picture of the face portrays the individual. The family continues
to be important all the time and accounts for much of the travelling we do.
We burst out, emigrate, go from east to west or from south to north, because
of the need to break away, and then we periodically travel back home just
to renew contacts. And we spend a lot of time writing letters, sending tele-
grams, telephoning, and hearing about our relations; moreover, in times of
stress, most people become loyal to the family setting and suspicious of the
foreigner.

Nonetheless, despite this common knowledge, the family is something that
deserves our detailed study. As a psycho-analyst, studying individual
emotional development in great detail, I have learned that each individual
needs to make the long road from being merged in with mother to being a
separate person, related to mother, and to mother and father together; from
here the journey goes through the territory known as the family, with father
and mother as the main structural features. The family has its own growth,
and the individual small child experiences the changes that belong to the
family's gradual expansion and to its troubles. The family protects the child
from the world. But gradually the world begins to seep in. The aunts and
uncles, the neighbours, the earliest sibling groups, leading on to schools. This
gradual environmental seeping-in is the way by which a child can best come
to terms with the wider world, and follows exactly the pattern of the infant's
introduction to external reality by the mother.

I know that our relations are often a nuisance, and that we are liable to
grumble because of the burden of them. We may even die of them. Yet they
are important to us. One has only to look at the struggles peculiar to men and
women with no relations at all (as, for instance, in the case of some refugees
and some illegitimate children) to see that the absence of relations to grumble
about, to love, to be loved by, to hate, and to fear, constitutes a terrible
handicap; it leads to a tendency to suspect even quite friendly neighbours.

What do we find when we begin to dissect some of the very real stresses which we encounter as soon as we begin to look below the surface?

POSITIVE TENDENCIES IN THE PARENTS

There comes a time after the marriage ceremony when it is very convenient if children begin to appear. If children come immediately they can very well be unwelcome, because the two young people have not yet passed through the initial stage in which they mean everything to each other. We all know of first children who by being born broke up the relationship between their fathers and mothers, and suffered on account of this. We also meet very many family settings in which children do not appear. Let us consider those cases in which children do appear and are a natural consequence of the relationship between the father and mother. Let us assume that the children are healthy. It has very often been said as a joke and with truth that children are a nuisance; but coming at the right time in a relationship they are the right kind of nuisance. There seems to be something in human nature that expects a nuisance, and it is better that this nuisance should be a child than an illness or an environmental disaster.

The existence of a family and the maintenance of a family atmosphere result from the relationship between the parents in the social setting in which they live. What the parents can 'contribute in' to the family that they are building up depends a great deal on their general relationship to the wider circle around them, their immediate social setting. One can think of ever-widening circles, each social group depending for what it is like inside on its relationship to another outside social group. Of course the circles overlap. Many a family is a going concern, yet would not stand being uprooted and transplanted.

But the parents cannot be considered simply in their relationship to society. There are powerful forces creating and binding the family in terms of the relationship between the parents themselves. These forces have been studied in great detail. They belong to the very complex fantasy of sex. Sex is not just a matter of physical satisfaction. I want especially to emphasize that sexual satisfactions are an achievement of personal emotional growth; when such satisfactions belong to relationships that are personally and socially agreeable they represent a peak of mental health. On the reverse side, disturbances in the sex field are associated with all manner of neurotic disorders, psychosomatic troubles, and wastage of the potential of the individual. However, although sex power is vitally important, complete satisfaction is not in itself an aim when the subject of the family is considered. It is worth noting that a large number of families exist and are counted good though they are built on a basis of not very powerful physical satisfactions on the

41

part of the parents. The extreme examples of physical satisfaction perhaps belong typically to romantic love, which is not *necessarily* the best basis for home-building.

Some people have but a poor capacity for the enjoyment of sex. Some frankly prefer auto-erotic experience, or homosexuality. However, it is obviously a very rich experience and fortunate for everyone concerned when the parents are able easily to enjoy the potency that belongs to individual emotional maturity. On top of this, we know that there are other things in the relationship between the parents which tend naturally towards the establishment of the family unit, such as the parents' deep-rooted wish to be like their own parents in the sense of being grown-up. We remember also the imaginative life, and such things as an overlap of cultural interests and pursuits.

Let us pause for a moment to consider that which I call 'the fantasy of sex'. Here I have to refer to matters that appear in the unusual frankness that belongs to psycho-analytic work. Psycho-analysis makes one wonder how a correct and adequate history of a marital case can be taken except as a by-product of a psycho-analytic treatment, or of the special conditions that go with psychiatric social work. The total sex fantasy, conscious and unconscious is almost infinitely variable, and has vital significance. It is important to understand, among other things, the sense of concern or guilt that arises out of the destructive elements (largely unconscious) that go along with the love impulse when this is expressed physically. It can be readily conceded that this sense of concern and guilt contributes a good deal to the need of each parent, and of the parents together, for a family. The growing family better than anything else *neutralizes the frightening ideas of harm done*, of bodies destroyed, of monsters generated. The very real anxieties in the father at the time of the mother's parturition reflect as clearly as anything else the anxieties that belong to the fantasy of sex and not just to the physical realities. Surely a great deal of the joy that the baby brings into the parents' lives is based on the fact that the baby is whole and human, and furthermore that the baby contains something that makes for living – that is to say, living apart from being kept alive; that the baby has an innate tendency towards breathing and moving and growing. The child *as a fact* deals, for the time being, with all the *fantasies* of good and bad, and the innate aliveness of each child gives the parents a great sense of relief as they gradually come to believe in it; relief from ideas that arise from their sense of guilt or unworthiness.

It is not possible to understand the attitude of parents to their children apart from a consideration of the meaning of each child in terms of the parents' conscious and unconscious fantasy around the act that produced the conception. Parents feel quite differently about, and act quite differently towards, each child. Much depends on the relationship between the parents at the time of conception, during the mother's pregnancy, at the time of the birth, and afterwards. The effect of the wife's pregnancy on her husband comes into this: in some extreme cases the husband turns from his wife when she becomes pregnant; sometimes he is drawn more closely to her. In every case there is an alteration in the relationship between the parents. often a great enrichment and a deepening of the sense of responsibility that each has for the other.

We hear it said that it is strange that children can be so different from each other when they have the same parents and are brought up in the same house and in the same home. This leaves out of account the whole of the imaginative elaboration of the important function of sex, and the way that each child fits specifically, or fails to fit, into a certain imaginative and emotional setting, a setting which can never be the same twice, even when everything else in the physical environment remains constant.

There are many other variations on this theme. Some are complex but some of them are obvious: for instance, whether the infant is a boy or a girl may profoundly affect the relationship between the parents. Sometimes it is a boy that is wanted by both; sometimes the mother feels frightened of her love of a boy baby, and becomes unable to allow the pleasure of the intimacy of breast-feeding on this account. Sometimes the father wishes for a girl and mother wishes for a boy, or the other way round.

It must be remembered that the family is composed of the individual children, each of whom is not only genetically distinct from the others but is also very much indeed influenced in his or her emotional growth by what I have referred to as the way in which the new child does or does not fit in with the parents' fantasy, which enriches and elaborates the physical relationship that they have, each in relation to the other. Always the most important thing in the whole of this is the tremendous reassurance that the live human infant brings through being a fact: real, and, as I have said, for the time being, neutralizing fantasy and eliminating expectations of disasters.

Those who have adopted children will know how such children can fill the gap in the imaginative needs arising out of a marriage. And married people with no children can and do find all sorts of other ways of in fact having a family; they may be found sometimes to have the largest families of all. But they would have preferred to have had their own born children.

What I have said so far, then, is that the two parents *need the actual children* in the development of their relationship each to the other, and the positive drives generated in this way are very powerful. It is not enough, for our intended purpose, to say that parents love their children. They often do get round to loving them, and they have all sorts of other feelings. Children need more of their parents than to be loved; they need something that carries over when they are hated and even hateful.

DISRUPTIVE FACTORS COMING FROM THE PARENTS

In considering the difficulties of parents, it is always valuable to remind ourselves that parents are not necessarily fully mature just because they have achieved marriage and the establishment of a family. Each member of the adult community is growing, and continues to grow, we hope, throughout life. But the adult has great difficulty in growing without throwing away the achievements of earlier stages of growth. It is easy for us to say that if people are mature enough to marry and have children they ought to be content to stay where they are and to cut their losses if they are not happy about themselves. Nevertheless, we know that in fact men and women have much growth to achieve in the decades that follow the time of their marriage if they marry at all early. Early is the best time for marriage, in terms of the establishment of a family. Children thrive best on parents who are twenty or thirty years older than themselves, and who are not too wise; such parents learn from their children and this has a lot to be said for it. Shall we hope that men and women will wait to marry until they are rich and perhaps smug? It is true, surely, that in the majority of cases men and women need to establish a platform (such as being married and having a family), and from this platform they eventually make further personal growth. They are often willing, easily willing, to wait for a number of years while their children are needing them for the family setting, and then they spurt forwards. Sometimes, however, there is a period of great strain before eventually the parents, or one parent, may re-start a new phase of growth.

It is indeed difficult to achieve full growth during adolescence. Society does not like free experiment among adolescents, and there are always those who like children to be nice. 'Nice' in adolescence means 'not thoughtlessly forming relationships'. The word 'thoughtlessly' here refers to careless pregnancies and illegitimate children. Many children pass through their adolescence in a somewhat inhibited way. In the case of immature men and women who marry, many find great relief and enjoyment in the establishment of a family; but we must not be surprised if ultimately the growth of their own children challenges them to go further with their own growth, which was held up at the time of their adolescence.

A social factor operates here. Big changes have taken place recently all over the world. If we are to have no more wars, then we will no longer have the distraction from adolescent problems that wars provided. So we find everywhere that adolescents are establishing adolescence as a phase in development that must be taken into account. It is essentially a phase of difficulty, a mixture of dependence and defiance, and the phase passes as the adolescent becomes adult. (Let us not be misled by the fact that new adolescents come along to keep the pot boiling.)

I would say that a great deal of what we see complicating family life is that which parents do when they come to the end of their ability to sacrifice everything for their children. Delayed adolescence in one or both parents is beginning to make itself felt. Perhaps this refers especially to the father because the mother so often discovers herself in the unexpected physical and emotional events that belong to motherhood. She too, however, may come at a later date to a tremendous need to experience romantic or passionate love which she avoided earlier because she wanted the right father for her children.

What now happens to the family? I am aware that in the vast majority of cases enough maturity exists in the parents for them to be able to make sacrifices themselves, as their parents did for them, in order to establish and maintain their family, so that the children may not only be born into a family but may grow and may reach adolescence in the family, and may in relation to the family pass right through to achieving an independent and perhaps married life, each one. But this is not always possible.

We should not, I think, despise those who were not very mature at the time of marriage and who cannot afford to wait indefinitely, and for whom the time comes when they must make new spurts forward in personal growth or else degenerate. Difficulties occur in the marriage, and the children then have to be able to adapt themselves to the family disruption. Sometimes parents are able to see children through to a satisfactory adult independence in spite of the fact that they themselves have found a necessity for breaking up the framework of a marriage, or perhaps have found a need for remarriage.

In a proportion of cases, of course, young married people deliberately avoid having children, knowing that, although they have reached something valuable by getting married, this is an unstable state of affairs; and knowing, each of them, that they may have to make new experiments before being ready to establish a family, which they intend to do eventually. They intend to establish a family partly because this is natural and partly because they hope to be like other parents and so to become socialized and integrated into the community. But a family is not the natural result of a romantic love affair. In the more unfortunate cases there is a state of chaos arising from difficulties of an extreme kind between the parents, difficulties which make it impossible for them to cooperate even in the care of children of whom they are fond.[1]

In this account I have deliberately omitted the disruptive effect of physical

[1] In Great Britain, since the Children Act of 1948, the state makes itself responsible for every child in England, Scotland, and Northern Ireland who is deprived of a home life, and this service is established throughout the country. Children's Departments seek first to maintain whenever possible each child's home life for him or her, and where this is not possible to place children in foster homes or to provide residential care for those who have special needs.

or mental illness[1] – but I have attempted to show how important is the study of the integrative and disintegrative factors making for family life or for its disruption: factors that come from the relationship between a man and a woman who have married, and from the conscious and unconscious fantasy of their sexual lives.

POSITIVE TENDENCIES IN THE CHILDREN

In considering the other half of the problem, that is to say, the integrative and disruptive factors relative to family life that come from the *children*, it must be remembered that each parent has been a child and to some extent is still a child.

It cannot be too strongly emphasized that the integration of the family derives from the integrative tendency of *each individual child*. Integration of the individual is not a thing that can be taken for granted. Personal integration is a matter of emotional growth. In the case of every human being a start has to be made from an unintegrated state. Much work has been done on this matter of the earliest stages in infant development, when the self is first becoming established and yet is still absolutely dependent on maternal care for making personal progress. In ordinary favourable conditions (which have to do with the mother's close identification with her child, and later on with the combined interest of the two parents), the human infant becomes able to give evidence of an innate tendency towards integration, this being part of the growth process. The process of growth must take place in the case of each child. If conditions are favourable at the earliest stages of great dependence, and an integration of the personality occurs, this integration of the individual, which is an active process involving fierce energies, affects the environment. The child who is developing well, and in particular whose personality has been able to achieve integration from within by the innate forces belonging to individual growth, has an integrative effect on the immediate environment; such a child 'contributes in' to the family situation.

This contributing in from each individual child may be forgotten until one experiences the shock of a child who is ill or defective, and who for one reason or another is not contributing in. One then observes how the parents and family suffer in consequence. Where the child is not contributing in the parents are burdened with a task which is not altogether a natural one – they have to supply a home setting and to maintain this setting, and to try to keep up a family and a family atmosphere *in spite of the fact that there is no help to be derived from the individual child*. There is a limit beyond which parents cannot be expected to succeed in such a task.

[1] The effects on the family of various types of mental illness are discusssd in Sections 7, 8, and 9 below.

Society depends on the integration of family units, but I think it is important to remember that these family units in turn depend on the integration which takes place in the growth of each individual member. In other words, in a healthy society, one in which democracy can flourish, a proportion of the individuals must have achieved a satisfactory integration *in their own personality development*. The idea of democracy and the democratic way of life arises out of the health and the natural growth of the individual, and can be maintained in no way except by the integration of the individual personality, multiplied of course many times according to the number of healthy or relatively healthy individuals that may exist in the community. There must be enough healthy individuals to carry the unintegrated personalities who cannot contribute in, otherwise society degenerates from a democracy.

It will be seen as a corollary of this that it is not possible *to make a community democratic*, since by undertaking the task of making the community democratic one is already applying a force *from outside* which is effective only if it comes from within, from each individual's health. However, a healthy society carries a proportion of passenger members. A healthy family too can carry children whose integrative tendencies are weak.

Each individual child, by healthy emotional growth and by the development of his or her personality in a satisfactory way, promotes the family and the family atmosphere. The parents, in their efforts to build a family, benefit from the sum of the integrative tendencies of the individual children. It is not just simply a matter of the lovableness of the infant or the child; there is something more than that, for children are not always sweet. The infant and the small child and the older child flatter us *by expecting a degree of reliability and availability* to which we respond, partly I suppose because of our capacity to identify with them. This capacity to identify with the children again depends on our having made a good-enough growth in our own personality development when we were at the same age. In this way, our own capacities are strengthened and are brought out, developed, by what is expected of us from our children. In innumerable and very subtle ways, as well as in obvious ways, infants and children produce a family around them, perhaps by needing something, something which we give because of what we know about expectation and about fulfilment. We see what the children create when playing at families, and we feel that we want to make real the symbols of their creativeness.

Parents are often able to fulfil the expectations of their children in a way or to a degree that is better than that which they experienced from their own parents. There is a danger here, however, that when they do better than their own parents beyond a certain degree, they inevitably begin to resent their own goodness, and indeed they tend to break up what they are doing so well. For this reason, some men and women can let themselves do better with children who are not their own than with their own children.

DISRUPTIVE FACTORS COMING FROM THE CHILDREN

From this one passes on to a consideration of the disintegration of the family brought about by a lack of development in the individual child or by the child's illness. In certain psychiatric illnesses of children there are tendencies of a secondary nature which develop and show themselves as an active need on the part of the child to break up anything that is good, stable, reliable, or in any way valuable. The outstanding example is the antisocial tendency of the deprived child who is most destructive of family life. The family, whether the child's own or a substitute family or community, constantly comes under test, and when tested and found reliable becomes the target of the child's destructive urges. This touches on the big problem of making provision for children with antisocial tendencies. It is as if the child is looking for something worth destroying. Unconsciously, the child seeks something good which has been lost at an earlier stage, and with which he is angry because it went. This is, of course, a separate subject, but it must be mentioned among all the patterns of disruption of family life that derive from the child's lack of development or distorted growth.

FURTHER DEVELOPMENT OF THE TWO THEMES

There is much that could be said about the interplay of all these various factors, factors that concern the parents and their relation to society and their wish to have a family, and factors that arise from the innate tendency towards integration which belongs to individual growth, but which – at any rate at the beginning – depends on the provision of a good-enough environment. There are many families which remain intact if the children happen to be developing well, but which cannot stand the presence in the family of an ill child.

In assessing a child with regard to suitability for psychotherapy, we find ourselves thinking not only of the diagnosis of the illness and of the availability of the psychotherapist, but also of the capacity of the family to tolerate, and in fact to 'hold', the child who is ill, and to tolerate the child's illness over the period of time before psychotherapy begins to take effect. In many cases it can be said that the family has to turn itself into a nursing home or even a mental hospital, in order to contain the illness or treatment of one of the children; and whereas many families are able to do this, in which case psychotherapy is a relatively simple matter, other families are unable to do so, and we then have to place the child away from the family. The task of psychotherapy in this case is very much more complex, and indeed it is exceedingly difficult to find suitable groups for the placement of children who are not able to contribute in. As the child has relatively little integrative tendency to bring to this group, the group must hold the child and the illness.

In many cases parents who are quite capable of producing healthy children and of giving them a good family setting do in fact find, for reasons which are not of the kind for which one could blame them, that they have in their midst an ill child, one who is anxious, or subject to psychosomatic disorder or to depression, or a child who is very much disintegrated in personality, or perhaps antisocial, and so on. It is then necessary either to ask the parents to nurse the difficult child while we try to help the child, or else, at the other extreme, to ask them to give up the task, letting them know in fact that although they can set up a home and maintain it for normal children, nevertheless the family that they have created is not able to tolerate this one particular child who is ill. They must be relieved of the responsibility for the time being. Often it happens that parents cannot stand being helped in this way, although they also cannot stand the alternative.

There are very difficult problems of management around this sort of case and these matters are mentioned here only to highlight the central theme, which is that it is something in the healthy development of every individual child that is at the basis of the integration of the family group. In the same way it is the healthy families, surely, that make possible the wider integrations, the wider groupings of all kinds, groupings which overlap and which are sometimes mutually antagonistic, and yet which can contain the germ of an ever-widening social circle.

The child cannot of course produce this family by magic – that is, without the parents and the parents' wish arising out of their own interrelationship. Nevertheless, each infant and child *creates* the family. It is true that parents bring about the existence of the family, but they need something from each infant and child – that which I am calling the individual child's creation. Failing this, the parents lose heart and will simply have a family setting unoccupied. They may of course adopt a child, or they may in some other way find indirect means of having the equivalent of a family. The strength of the family comes from its being a meeting-place between something that arises out of the relationship of the father and the mother, and something that derives from the innate factors that belong to the emotional growth of the individual child – factors which I have put together under the heading of a tendency towards integration.

7

The Family Affected by Depressive Illness in one or both Parents

In the previous section I looked at some of the factors, in both parents and children, that make for the disruption of family life. I propose to follow up this general theme in the next three sections, by considering the disintegration of the family that may be brought about by psychiatric illness. When we are called upon to help in situations where there is evidence of failure in the family dynamics, we seek to understand the factors underlying the difficulties with which we are presented, in order that our help may be of the most appropriate kind. We are not concerned with making moral judgements in these matters; nor am I thinking, in this context, in terms of the problem of economic strain – which in any case is rarely found to be the sole source of stress.

Here I will examine the effect on the family of depressive illness in one or both parents. First, I refer briefly to the characteristics of certain forms of psychiatric illness.

CLASSIFICATION OF PSYCHIATRIC DISORDER

Psychiatric illness can be artificially divided into two kinds, psychoneurosis and psychosis. Psychosis has to do with madness or an element of madness hidden within the personality. Psychoneurosis takes its pattern from the defences organized in the intact individual personality, warding off or dealing with anxiety that arises out of the fantasy or the actual in interpersonal relationships. Psychoneurotic disorder in the father or mother provides a complication for the growing child, but psychosis in a parent presents the child with more subtle threats to healthy development.

By the term psychosis[1] I refer to a deeper line of defence, to the changes that take place in the individual's personality in the face of strain that it is beyond the capacity of the individual to deal with by ordinary defence mechanisms, perhaps because the strain and the pattern of the strain occurred too early.

---

[1] Psychotic illness in parents and children, and its effect on family life, is the subject of Sections 8 and 9 below.

The extreme of psychosis is the mental hospital case. A very severe psychotic breakdown is rather like a physical illness in the sense that it is easily recognized as an illness, and the medical profession knows how to take responsibility when confronted with such obvious disorder.

Depression, which is my subject here, is an affective or mood disorder, but there are two special states that I want to refer to at this point.

One is the psychopathic personality – here we are concerned mainly with fathers, whereas depression chiefly concerns mothers. The psychopath is an adult who has not recovered from a delinquency of childhood. This delinquency was originally (in the history of the individual) an antisocial tendency in a deprived child. The deprivation at the beginning was real and was perceived as such by the child; it was a loss of something that was good, and I am intending to imply that something happened, after which nothing was the same again. The antisocial tendency therefore represented a compulsion in the child to make external reality mend the original trauma, which of course quickly became forgotten and therefore became unmendable by simple reversal. In the psychopath this compulsion to go on forcing external reality to make good its failure continues, and we are often caught up in the problems produced by the effects of this compulsion in one or both parents.

The other is the particular twist that may accompany depression or the antisocial tendency, which has to do with delusions of persecution, or suspicion. This tendency to feel persecuted is a complication of depression, and on the whole it makes the depression less obvious as such, because this bit of madness (the delusion of persecution) side-tracks the sense of guilt which is characteristic of the melancholic and the depressive. Those who are ill in this way alternate between on the one hand feeling ridiculously that they are bad, and on the other hand feeling madly, insanely, that they are ill-treated. In either case we may find that we can do nothing to bring about a cure; we have to accept the condition. It is more hopeful when depression is not complicated by suspicion and delusions of persecution, for in these more normal cases the individual displays some flexibility and an easier alternation between a depressed mood and a sense of something external being a bad influence or a persecuting agent.

DEPRESSION IN THE MOTHER OR THE FATHER

I come now to the subject of depression. This is more interesting because it is more closely related to ordinary life. For although at one end of the scale there is melancholia, at the other end there is depression, a condition which is common to all integrated human beings. When Keats said of the world: 'Where but to think is to be full of sorrow and leaden-eyed despair', he did not mean that he was of no value or even that he was in an ill state of mind. Here was someone who took the risk of feeling things deeply and of taking responsibility. At the one extreme, therefore, are the melancholics, who take responsibility for all the ills of the world, especially those which are quite obviously nothing to do with them, and at the other extreme are the truly responsible people of the world, those who accept the fact of their own hate, nastiness, cruelty, things which coexist with their capacity to love and to construct. Sometimes their sense of their own awfulness gets them down.

If we look at depression in this way we can see that it is the really valuable people in the world who get depressed, including the fathers and mothers of families. It is perhaps a pity that they suffer from depression, but to be not able to doubt or to suffer dismay is a worse condition. And the forced gaiety that indicates denial of depression becomes boring after a time even if it has its place at a Christmas party.

There is no sharp line between a mother's or father's despair about a child and a general doubt about life and the purpose of life. In practice one sees the shift to and fro from concern to despair, and it is sometimes just a little bit of help from a friend or a doctor that makes the difference for the time being between hope and despair in an individual's life. Perhap what I have said will have linked up common depression with the ordinary experience of life. I know that depression can be a crippling illness, calling for treatment, but much more commonly it is just what all of us feel like every now and again. We do not want to be jogged or jigged out of our mood, but a real friend tolerates us, helps us a little, and waits.

I have had opportunity for the observation of depression in mothers and fathers because of having an outpatients' clinic of my own in a children's hospital over a period of thirty years. Thousands of mothers have attended this clinic and the children have had every kind of disorder, physical and psychological. Often the child is not ill, but it is the mother who *today* is worried about her child; *tomorrow* perhaps she is not worried though she ought to be. I quickly learned to think of my clinic as a department for the management of maternal and paternal hypochondria. (Naturally, of course, it was chiefly the mothers who brought the children, but by no means always, and I leave out fathers only for the sake of convenience.)

It is important for mothers to be able to bring their children to the doctor when they are somewhat depressed. They may of course go to an adult clinic and express concern about their internal organs or about some part of their body that is not completely healthy. They may possibly go to a psychiatrist and openly complain of depression. They may consult a priest because of their doubts about their goodness; or they may try a quack nostrum. The fact is that the sense of *doubt* is very close to its opposite which is *belief*, and to a sense of values, and to the feeling that *there are things worth preserving*.

In drawing attention therefore to depression I refer not only to a severe psychiatric illness but also to a phenomenon which is almost universal among healthy people and which is closely linked with their capacity when not depressed to do a good job.

One of the jobs that people find themselves doing is setting up and maintaining a family. The family therefore is one of the things which may find itself in jeopardy when the husband or wife is depressed. Let me give an example:

A mother brings a boy to the clinic because she notices that he has gone thin in the week before the consultation. It is clear to me that this woman is chronically depressed, and I take it for granted that for the time being she is worried about her boy and that this gives her some relief because usually she is worried vaguely about herself. I find through my contact with the boy that his illness started with a very severe example in the family life of the recurring clashes between the father and mother at a point when the father suddenly asked the two children: 'Do you wish to live with me or with mother?' – implying that he and the mother intended to separate. The father does in fact ill-treat his wife constantly. The father is immature and feckless, and quite happy. But here I am concerned with the mother and her chronic depressive state.

What is my treatment of this woman's concern about her child's loss of weight? In my clinic the treatment is not to deal with the mother's depression by psychotherapy but to examine the boy. Usually I find no illness. I choose this case because this boy in fact had started diabetes. My objective study of the boy's condition and the subsequent treatment of the boy were what the mother needed. She will continue to be ill-treated by her husband. She will continue to be chronically depressed and sometimes deeply depressed. But within the limits of the problem presented I dealt with her worry. Naturally, the boy besides being treated for his diabetes was given help in regard to the understanding of the home situation. I am not surprised, however, to find that what I do does not clear up the bigger problem, which is the mother's chronic depression.

THE LIMITED LIABILITY IN SOCIAL WORK

In many cases it is possible to deal successfully with depression in a mother by examining the thing that is worrying her and dealing with that thing. For instance, she may have got into a muddle in her housekeeping, and have inadvertently got into debt, in spite of having a strong dislike of dishonesty; or perhaps her husband has been out of work and she is unable to pay the TV instalments.

Another mother brings her little girl to me and it is not clear why she has brought her. One could almost say that the symptoms complained of depend on the department that she happens to reach. She might have asked a throat and nose surgeon whether the child's adenoids needed attention. She might have asked an eye surgeon if he thought that the child was seeing well. She can quickly follow the expectations of a physician and describe any symptoms that seem to interest the doctor. I am able to take a careful history and this gives the mother some insight into her own fluctuations in her attitude to the child. She can see that on the whole the child is developing well in spite of the fact that from time to time the mother becomes worried about her daughter. The girl does have some symptoms, and these include some loss of appetite.

In this case I decide that my job is to say to the mother something like this: 'You were right to bring the child when you felt worried about her; that is what we are for; at the present time in my opinion this child is quite healthy and I am willing to reconsider my opinion next week or when you feel like coming again.'

Here the mother has received the reassurance that she needs by my examination of the child and by the fact that I take what she says seriously. She finds it difficult to believe that the child is well, but tomorrow perhaps she will have forgotten her anxiety. It would be quite useless for a doctor to say to such a mother that she is a silly old fusspot, especially when she is!

Furthermore, it is important to remember, where there is psychiatric illness in the parents, that if we are felt to be a support in the home we must be prepared to be 'on the side of the home against' authority, or against whatever agency has become anathema to the mother or father.

We may sometimes wonder why it is that people such as those I have described just fail to get help by natural means, so that accumulation of muddle and despair builds up into paralysis. In ordinary life a friend would have done the sort of thing which we do in our professional relationship. But some people do not make friends easily. Often the people with whom we work are suspicious. They keep themselves to themselves, or they are withdrawn, or perhaps they have moved to a different locality once or twice or three times, and they have no technique for making contact with neighbours. People can usually find a way around minor difficulties, but only too easily a failure activates a latent depression, and just not being able to pay an instalment on a hire-purchase contract may rouse despair about life and the meaning of life. Something has been touched off that belongs to very much deeper matters than the acquisition of a TV set.

What we are doing, it is clear, does not concern the day-to-day management only, but day-to-day management is one of the methods that people employ in their fight against depression. Successful management of one day means hope; but just a little muddle, and what is felt is the threat of a completely chaotic state from which there could be no recovery.

SOCIAL WORK THERAPY

In much of our professional work we are being psychotherapists, though we are not making interpretations of the unconscious. We are dealing with people's depressions, preventing depressions and helping people out of them. We are mental nurses. In mental hospitals the mental nurse's trouble is that success is so difficult to attain. Fortunately we often have a chance to succeed. The strain of the mental nurse is the toleration of failure, which is so very much a part of his or her job. How the mental nurse in the mental hospital must envy us for the chance that we have to succeed because we are in touch with depression at the end of the scale at which there is a tendency to self-cure, and this tendency can frequently be helped and hastened by some little thing that we do. At the same time we must recognize that in our work we too may have severe cases, and we too have to tolerate failure, and we certainly have to know how to wait before we can be sure that a result has been obtained. As a psycho-analyst I have had very good training in this matter of waiting and waiting and waiting. There are also those successes which do not look like successes on paper – when we feel sure that what we did was worth while, although perhaps in the end the man went to prison again, or the woman committed suicide, or the children eventually were taken into care or became probation cases.

What is the difference between the hopeless mental hospital case and the hopeful depression which we are often able to help? There is no essential difference in the psychology of the two types of case. The melancholic in the hospital, unable to do anything at all for months or even years, strikes her breast with her fists and says: 'Woe is me!'; she is unable to worry about something in particular because she cannot get near the true cause. Instead of that she feels unlimited guilt, and she suffers and continues to suffer, and in the end we all suffer because of her suffering. Sometimes she says that she has killed someone dear to her, or that it is her fault that there was a train disaster in Japan. It is of no avail if we argue the case. Our breath is wasted.

The rather more hopeful cases, on the other hand, are those in which the woman who is in a state of depression is able to be depressed *about* something, something that has some sense in it. She is worried about not being able to keep the house clean. Here we can well understand that there is a build-up, with reality interwoven with fantasy; the depression makes it difficult for her to get the work done, and the work getting behindhand makes her depressed.

There is something hopeful about a case, if the depression takes the form of a worry *about* something. This gives us a way in. It is *not* our job to try to

mediate problem. There is an economics in our work and we can do what we have to do if we do the right thing at the right moment; but if we attempt the impossible the result is that we become depressed ourselves and the case remains unaltered.

Let me now give two more examples:

Here is a very good family consulting me in private practice. There is a strong family tradition, and the family lives in a beautiful house and grounds, and there is every material advantage. One of two boys is brought to me because the parents can see that he is developing in a false way. His manners are perfect, and somehow or other what he has lost is childhood.

The point that I want to make is this, that I saw both the boys, several times, and gradually I found that it was necessary to get them looked after by someone other than the mother. The mother is dealing with depression in herself. She is having some treatment and no doubt she will come through; but my treatment of these boys, which so far has been rather successful, has left this mother with a terrible sense of being a failure. It has been traumatic for her that she has had to allow someone else to look after her two sons. What she does now is to worry about her absolutely normal daughter. She asks me to give my attention now to this child, and it is important that I let her know from to time that I nave considered this next child from all angles and that I am willing to reconsider the case, but that at the moment all I can see is a normal child. Any doubt that I might express would be translated by this mother as a confirmation of her own anxieties that she is really no good at all. She is of course a very good person, and she and her husband have built a home which will last and which will be able to see all the children right through till they have emerged from adolescence into that independence which we begin to call adult life. This mother saw me since I wrote this. She is having treatment and is much less depressed than she was. She said: 'The house has been done up and this means that a crack in the ceiling of one room is now no longer a feature. The little girl went in and said: "Isn't it lovely now there's no crack." ' (She has been in terror of this crack.) I said to the mother: 'Your child has evidently noticed your own improvement.'

A colleague of mine resisted psychological matters for a long time. He was a surgeon and it surprised him himself, I think, when he one day said to me that he wanted me to see his children because they seemed to be full of symptoms. What I found was a healthy family life with quite a lot of strain between the parents but a stability which was sufficient. The symptoms of the children were of the kind that belong to their age, and we know what a lot of symptoms children can have when they are two, three, and four years old. I nearly missed the point in this case, which was the depression in the father, which was taking the form of a doubt about his capacity to be a husband and a father. Fortunately I saw this just in time and I said to him: 'These children are what I call normal.' His relief was tremendous and lasting, and the family has grown and prospered. It would have been disastrous if, after seeing the anxieties and difficulties in these children's lives and in the relationship between the parents, I had started to try to clear them up. I had a limited task and I think in this case I did the thing I had to do well, but it had to be done quickly, without delay, and with a quiet certainty. I think that even an intelligence test, any expression of doubt on my part, would have made this case into a very complex matter for management over a long period. I know how this man's wife would have hated it if I had suggested that the children should have psychotherapy.

At this point I would draw attention to the quantity of depression which can be contained by the individual, without others being severely hurt. Here is a case in illustration:

It concerns a woman who is particularly brilliant in the intellectual field and who could certainly have taken a very responsible post in education. She chose to marry, however, and she has brought up three children, three boys who are now married; she has eight grandchildren. One can say that her life has been markedly successful, especially in this matter of the bringing up of children and the establishment of a family. She has been able to bear the premature death of her husband and to avoid leaning too heavily on her children when, as a widow, she finds herself needing to go to work in order to occupy her energies and to earn her living. Now this woman, I happen to know, suffers from a very severe depression every morning. This has been a feature of her life. From waking in the morning until she has had breakfast and made herself look like something that the world might accept she is in the very deepest depression, and not only crying but also in danger at times of suicidal impulse.

I think that one can say that she is as ill, between waking and breakfast, as many melancholics in mental hospitals. She has suffered intensely. No doubt her family would have managed even better had she not had this illness to contend with. Nevertheless, in her case, as in the case of so many other people, the depression has been a self-contained thing, mainly felt by herself, and as far as possible she has come to terms with the fact that life for her is like that. During the rest of the day one would hardly know anything about her except that she is a very valuable person and that her sense of responsibility is something which is just what children need in order to feel secure.

These rather more normal people with depressions have friends, however.

Their friends know about them, and are fond of them and value them, and are therefore able to give them the sort of support which is necessary. But what about those individuals who also have some difficulty in regard to the making of friends and the use of neighbours? This is the complication which makes it necessary for us to come in, in a professional way, giving the same sort of help that a friend would give, but in a professional manner and in a limited sense. This same suspicion which makes friendships difficult will also often interfere with the person's ability to make use of us professionally. Or else we may find that we are accepted as a friend and idealized so that all the time we have to hear someone else being denigrated, either some other social worker, or the local authority, or the housing committee, or the dark people who have a flat downstairs, or the in-laws. Here is a paranoid system, in which we happen to be the right side of the line that separates good from bad. When we are on the bad side we may become excluded.

PSYCHOLOGY OF DEPRESSION

I conclude with a brief account of the psychology of depression. This is, of course, a highly complex subject, and, moreover, there are various kinds of depression:

    severe melancholia;
    depression alternating with mania;
    depression showing as denial of depression (hypomanic state);
    chronic depression, with more or less paranoid anxiety;
    depression phases in normal people;
    reactive depression, which is allied to mourning.

There are certain common features in all these clinical states. The main thing is that depression indicates that the individual is accepting responsibility for the aggressive and destructive elements in human nature. This means that the depressed person has a capacity for holding a certain amount of guilt (about matters that are chiefly unconscious), and this allows of a searching round for an opportunity for constructive activity.

Depression is evidence of growth and health in the emotional development of the individual. When the very early stages of emotional development are not satisfactorily achieved, then the individual does not get so far as to feel depressed. My meaning will be clearer, perhaps, if I refer to the development of a sense of concern. If all goes well in individual growth, and only if all goes well, the little child at some stage begins to become concerned about himself or herself, and about the results of loving. Loving is not just a matter of affectionate contact. Loving has to gather to itself the instinctual urges which have a biological backing to them, and the relationship that develops between an infant and a mother (or a father or someone else) carries with it destructive ideas. It is not possible to love freely and fully without having ideas that are destructive. The achievement of a sense of guilt about these destructive ideas and urges that go along with loving is followed by the urge to give and to repair, and to love in a more adult way. ('Loving', of course, has parallel with it 'being loved'.) Opportunity for constructive activity is part and parcel of this individual growth process and is intimately connected with the capacity to feel guilt and doubt and to be depressed.

Much is always unconscious, however, and depression as a mood reflects this fact, that much is unconscious. When the aggression and the destructiveness that are part of human nature, and the ambivalence, as it is sometimes called, in human relationships – when these things have been reached in personal development, but have become deeply repressed and inaccessible, then we get melancholia turning up as an illness. In such illness the sense in the sense of guilt that is the crippling agent is no longer available, except through a long and deep psycho-analytic treatment.

It is important to remember, however, that since there is some health where there is depression, so depression tends to cure itself, and often a little help from outside makes all the difference and helps the depression to lift. The basis for this help is acceptance of the depression, not an urge to cure it. It is just where the individual can allow us to see a place where we can help that we have our chance to give indirect help, remembering that what we are really engaged in is mental nursing in a case of depression.

8

The Effect of Psychosis on Family Life

Perhaps I had better first try to explain what the word psychosis means to me. Psychosis is an illness of a psychological nature, but it is not psychoneurosis. In some cases it has a physical basis (e.g. arterio-sclerosis). It is an illness of persons, and the persons concerned are not healthy enough to be psychoneurotic. It would simplify things if we could say that psychosis means 'very ill' and psychoneurosis 'rather ill'; but the complication here is that healthy people can play about with psychosis, whereas this does not often happen with psychoneurosis. Psychosis is much more down to earth and concerned with the elements of human personality and existence than is psychoneurosis, and (to quote myself!) we are poor indeed if we are only sane.

Psychosis can be thought of as a popular term for schizophrenia, for manic depression, and for melancholia with more or less paranoid complication. There is no sharp line between any one illness and another, and it often happens that someone who is obsessional, for instance, becomes depressed or confused, and returns to being obsessional. Here psychoneurotic defences change over into psychotic defences and back again. Or schizoid persons become depressives. Psychosis represents an organization of defences, and behind all organized defences there is the threat of confusion, in fact a breakdown of integration.

What the effect of psychosis can be on family life is most clearly shown from a discussion of actual cases. Those of us who are concerned with these problems are aware that many families break up because of the strain of psychosis in one of their members, and that most of these families would probably remain intact if they could be relieved of such intolerable strain. This is an immense practical problem and there is acute need for preventive measures, especially in the form of the provision of mental hospital care for children. I think in terms of a residential centre where children could be kept for an indefinite period, and from which they could be taken for daily treatment by psycho-analysts, who would at the same time be treating other types of patient, including adults.

The problems presented by psychosis merge into those produced by primary mental defect, by physical defect such as spastic diplegia and allied disorders, by the after-effects of encephalitis (happily less common now than in the 1920s), and by the various clinical forms of the antisocial tendency indicating deprivation. However, for my purpose here, psychosis proper would indicate a disturbance of emotional development at an early level, the brain being intact. In some cases a hereditary tendency to psychosis is strong, whereas in others it is not a significant feature.

I begin with a case that I have watched for many years without making any difference to the situation.

A boy was born to a rather masculine woman, and he turned out to be a sort of caricature of his father. His father was highly dependent on his wife, made few decisions, and took but little responsibility. Nevertheless he was able to earn a good living as an expert in a highly specialized subject. The boy showed early signs of having a very good brain and of being psychotic. His disorder was not early recognized because every sign could be seen as a reproduction of the father's childhood characteristics. The grandmother would always say: 'But the boy's father did that.' For instance, in character-istic psychotic fashion he came to his grandmother in the drawing-room and said: 'You've dirtied your pants.' His father got things the wrong way round, too, and had said the same when he was a boy.

Whereas the father's specializations had turned out to be fruitful, the boy's were dead ends. For instance, he classified thirty-eight kinds of traffic signal in London. He just missed specializing usefully. Of course he could not do sums because he did not know what ONE meant, but with luck he might have by-passed sums and stepped over into higher mathematics, or he might have become a chess prodigy. But he did not. He is now thirty years old. These parents have had to orientate themselves to the immediate problems, and also to the future. They have saved in order to leave money for his care. They have not dared to have more children. More than that, they might have grown up themselves, as many do, and late in life perhaps they might have parted and each re-started a rather more mature kind of marriage. But psychosis in the midst held these two responsible people in a vice. From this there is no escape.

In giving this case history I have slipped in some personal views on marriage and re-marriage. There are those who quite genuinely believe in growing up; such people, having missed adolescence, will if necessary go through it somewhere in mid-life.[1] The question is: how much distress is involved to be counterbalanced by advantages? When psychosis or a similar disorder dominates the scene there may be no alternative to going on coping, except, perhaps, for the feckless.

[1] For fuller discussion of this theme, see Section 6 above.

Here is another long-term case:

I was consulted about a boy of 7½, an only child, born with evidence of head-damage. By the time of the consultation he was thought to be mentally defective but he displayed many signs of being clever. He became able to read at about eight simply because he had a nurse who said she would get him to read even if it did him harm. Being able to read was important and afforded his parents some relief. The boy (now twenty) started to present problems quite early. He was an only child and probably a mistake. I guess these parents never intended to have a child, or they were not ready. They were fully occupied with work and horses and things; their idea of life was to have a few days and nights of concentrated office work midweek, living in a small tidy flat, sandwiched between weekends in the heart of England with life in the raw, all mixed up with foxes and hunt balls. It was at weekends that these two people lived.

Now put into this a psychotic boy who screams all night, who makes messes and wets, and who has no use for the country at all, is scared of dogs, and will not sit on a horse. It just does not work.

These very good people had to make a most artificial adjustment to a life that would suit the boy, and of course nothing suited him. They sacrificed a great deal to get him some treatment, but this did not cure him. The father died prematurely of a stroke while at the height of his career, and the mother is left stranded, with sole responsibility for this boy. A school has come to the rescue, and the boy stays on there, although unable to become a mature person to whom some responsibility could be given. The worst part is that the boy is a very lovable person that one could not hurt, and he will always be needing the attention that it is easy to give to a normal child of five, but not so easy to give to any one child for ever.

Now let me choose a more hopeful case:

A little boy of highly responsible parents started to go backwards instead of forwards in his development at a certain point which seemed to coincide with the mother's pregnancy. A thoroughgoing childhood psychosis developed, and till recently this boy would have been thought to be defective.

Here it was possible to arrange a psychotherapy, and the treatment has proved moderately successful. The parents have done everything possible to support this treatment and to wait for results, but they could not have kept the home together had it not been for an arrangement made through the hospital almoner, whereby the child has been called for at a certain time by car several times a week (already for two years) and transported about twenty miles and back. The expense has been enormous but surely justified.

In this particular case the family was just able to stand the illness of the child. I would mention here that a successful treatment of a child can be traumatic for one or both of the parents. The latent psychosis in the adult which was doing quite well, hidden and asleep, springs to life because of the child's deep changes towards health, and starts clamouring for recognition and attention. In the following case a boarding school accepted the child:

A headmaster of a public school had a son of his own who nearly wrecked his career, which was serious since he simply was not fitted for any other. The boy, the last of several children (the older children were normal), developed a confusional state, and this persisted, making him impossible at his own school in the town and in the school where he lived at night. He was entirely restless and unpredictable. His mother might have managed one more *normal* child but she was too old to deal with this last one, whose state was incompatible with restfulness. The father kept to his study and to his routine, and he looked on at a distance, as if through the wrong end of a telescope.

This mother has tremendous drive and she is always trying to organize help for parents who find themselves in a plight like hers. The family would have broken up but for the fact that a school took this boy and accepted him as he was, without expecting that he would be an asset. He is now nearly twenty and still at school.

More and more boarding schools tend to want their boys and girls to do well, or else they are schools designed to take maladjusted children. This boy was not maladjusted, and he showed no antisocial tendency; he is affectionate and always expecting to be liked. But he is often confused, or at best organized into several dissociated pieces. Could he have treatment? I saw him several times, but I could not find any place to put him and keep him while coming to me or to a colleague every day.

Cases such as these do badly because they have not that property of the antisocial tendency which goes on and on until it *makes* some authority put a ring round them, emotional or physical. This boy's illness just goes on wearing down the family structure and the boy does not even get pleasure or benefit from trying or succeeding or failing. The other children in such a family get away as soon as possible, and the ageing parents wilt, worrying about what will happen after they crack up. It makes no difference if it was something in the parents that caused the child's illness. Often this is the case. But the damage was done neither wilfully nor wantonly. It just happened.

A north-country professor and his wife had a good family set-up and all was well till a childhood psychosis, built on an undetected infantile cretinism, came and disturbed them. They simply could not cope with the psychotic illness of their girl child.

I was fortunate in this instance in being able to exploit a friendship with a Children's Officer – with the result that a foster home was quickly found for this girl, a working-class family in a country district in southern England. Here in the family the backward but developing child could be accepted as convalescent from illness. The professor's family was saved by this device, and the professor was able to go ahead in his career. I was interested in the fact that the difference in the social status of the parents and foster parents did not seem to matter, and certainly it was important for this little girl that no one expected her to be academically bright. Moreover, I was glad that there was this distance between the home and the foster home.

There is so often this complication, that parents feel guilty about their child's condition. They could not explain it but they cannot separate off the child's condition from expected retribution. The foster parents have no burden of this kind, and so they are more free to accept the child as rude, odd, backward, incontinent, dependent.

However obvious it may be, I want to make this observation again: no family should be allowed to crack up because of psychosis in a child or parent. At any rate we should be able to *offer* relief, which at present we usually cannot do.

I do not know why it is that most of the examples that have sprung to my mind have been of boy children. Is this just chance, or is there some way that girls have of hiding themselves better, of putting on an act, looking like mother, and all the time preserving their identity like an unborn baby inside them? I think there is a little truth in the theory that a girl can get away with a false self, one that complies and copies, better than a boy can; that is to say, a girl can more easily avoid being taken to a child psychiatrist. It is probable that the psychiatrist comes into his own here when the girl develops anorexia or colitis or is a nuisance in adolescence, or becomes a depressive young adult.

A thirteen-year-old girl was brought a hundred miles to see me, sent by the local authority which had come to the end of its resources. I saw in the waiting-room a highy suspicious girl, with a father ready to explode over me. It was necessary for me to act quickly and I told the father to wait (poor man!), and saw the girl for an hour. In this way, by taking her side, I was able to make a deep contact with her which lasted for years, and could still be used. I had to collude with her paranoid delusions about her family. Those delusions were wrapped up in facts about her family which were probably accurate.

After an hour she could let me see her father, who was right up on his high horse and on the defensive, he being an important figure in local government and his position being completely undermined by what the girl was telling everybody. The political position of the father made it almost impossible for the local authority to act as it wished to do, and indeed there was no clear answer to the problem.

The only thing I could do was to say that this girl *must never go home again*. On this basis she had a year or two at a home with a remarkable matron, where she was happy and where she could be trusted with the care of small children.

Eventually, however, it was the girl who started going home, and it is likely that an unconscious tie-up existed with the mother, unconscious on both sides; soon troubles re-started.

The next I heard was that she was at an approved school, along with a lot of young prostitutes. She stayed there a year or two but did not become a prostitute because she was not a deprived child with an antisocial tendency. The compulsively heterosexual girls around her used to laugh at her for having no street life.

But this girl was still acutely paranoid. She created jealousy situations and ran away. She was eventually sent to a hostel for the maladjusted, and then she became a nurse. She would ring me up, anytime, and tell me she was in trouble at the hospital. The matrons and sisters were nice, and they liked her work and the patients liked her; but there were things wrong that would catch up on her – lies she had told in order to get the job, past payments not made to the various health and unemployment funds – but she knew I could do nothing, and eventually she would ring off; and then again, the same story at another hospital, and the same hopelessness. A haunted soul she remained, and the basis of my relationship to her was that I said: 'You must never ever go home again.' But no one who lived near the girl's home could have said this, because of course it was not really a bad home, and if the girl had lost her paranoid illness she would have been able to see her home as quite tolerable, as homes go.

Psychotic illness in a parent often defeats us just because the responsibility lies with the ill persons. It is not always true that there is one healthy parent to carry on, and it may easily be that the healthy parent gets out to save his or her own sanity, even at the cost of leaving a child in the grip of the psychosis of the other parent.

In this next case, there was illness in the parents:

It concerns a boy and a girl, with only a year between their ages. The girl is older, which was in itself a disaster here. They were the only children of two very ill people. The father was highly successful in business and the mother was an artist who sacrificed her career by marrying. The mother was quite unsuitable for being a mother, being a hidden schizophrenic. She took a deep breath and married, and had these two children in order to socialize herself in her family circle. Her husband was a manic-depressive character and a near psychopath.

As soon as the boy was 'clean' the mother could stand him; she had no use for babies. She made continuous and violent love to her boy, though not physically as far as I know, and he had a schizophrenic breakdown in adolescence. The girl was much affected by a powerful attachment to her father, and this gave her a second chance; on this basis she waited till she was forty and her parents were dead before she could break down. Meanwhile she became a successful businesswoman, carrying on her father's work after his death. She had a contempt for men, and knew of 'no reason why they should be thought superior', and she proved in her work that she lacked nothing, whereas her brother lacked everything a male needs. The brother married, had a family, and then got rid of his wife so that he could mother his children, which he did excellently.

Eventually, all the past having been blotted out, this very ill person with a successful false self came for a treatment. She came to be enabled to break down, to find her own schizophrenia, which she succeeded in doing. The doctor who sent her to me was not impressed when I wrote him a letter, before starting to treat her, saying that if the treatment went well she would break down and need care. Well, she got herself certified, and then quickly gathered herself together and was decertified and discharged before she could be got at by shocks and leucotomies, which she intelligently hated.

So here was a parental psychosis working itself out in two very clever children who are now nearly forty-five. The woman may perhaps have some life to lead as a real person, I am not sure yet. (Follow up: favourable.)

If another case like this should come to me, I shall wisely let someone else become responsible for helping the patient to break down. But I am glad I witnessed the relief that such a breakdown can give to a person with a built-up false self of extreme degree.

The question is: what can we learn from this brief case description? The point may be that there was no possible relief for this girl till her parents had died and she was established as an independent unit. The cost of waiting was tremendous; she felt futile and unreal, except for occasional glimpses of the real which she got through the visual arts and through music.

It is a terrible thing, and yet it is true, that sometimes there is no hope for the children till the parents have died. Psychosis in these cases is in the parent,[1] and its grip on the child is such that the only hope is the development

---

[1] See also Section 9 below.

of a false self; and of course the child may die first, but at any rate the child's true self has preserved its integrity, hidden away, and safe from violation.

These case histories reveal something of the despair that cannot be avoided in the course of clinical work with people. Sometimes, when confronted with severe illness, we have to let things be, and wait until perhaps the family cracks up under the strain; sometimes it is our task to break up a situation before it deteriorates further; in other cases we try to deal with the existing confusion. All too often we can find no grounds for hope, and this we need to be able to accept, for we do no good to anyone if we ourselves become paralysed by despair.

9

The Effect of Psychotic Parents on the Emotional Development of the Child

In our consideration of psychosis and family life in the previous section, most of the cases were described in terms of the problems created by psychotic illness in the child. I now want to examine further the effect of psychosis in the parent on the emotional development of the child and on the family.

As a starting-point, I will try to convey something of the beauty of a poem written by an eleven-year-old girl. I cannot reproduce the poem here because it has been published elsewhere over the girl's own name, but it gives in a sequence of economical short lines a perfect picture of home life in a happy family setting. The feeling conveyed is of a family of children of various ages, the children interacting with each other, jealousies being experienced but tolerated, the family pulsating with potential living. In the end night comes, and the atmosphere is handed over to the dogs and the owls and to the world outside the house. Inside all is quiet, safe, and still. The poem gives the impression that it comes right out of the life of the young authoress. How else, one wonders, could she possibly know these things?

The Story of Esther
Let me call the authoress Esther, and ask: what is Esther's background? She is the foster child of intelligent middle-class parents who have an adopted son and now have another fostered girl. The father has always been devoted to Esther and he is very sensitive in his understanding of her. The question is, what is this child's early history, and how does she come to the serenity of this poem, full of the atmosphere and the details of family life?

Esther's real mother was said to be a very intelligent woman, who was at ease in several languages; but her marriage came to grief, and then she lived with a 'tramp-type'. Esther was the illegitimate result of this union. In her early months, therefore, Esther was left with a mother who was entirely on her own. The mother was the last but one of many children. During her pregnancy, it was recommended to the mother that she should have treatment as a voluntary boarder, but she did not accept this suggestion. The

69

mother nursed the child herself from birth, and she is described, in a social worker's report, as idolizing her baby.

This state of affairs continued until Esther was five months old, when the mother began to behave strangely, and to look wild and vague. After a sleepless night she wandered in a field near a canal, watching an ex-police constable digging. She then walked to the canal and threw the baby in. The ex-police constable rescued the infant immediately, unharmed, but the mother as a result of this was detained, and was subsequently certified as a schizophrenic with paranoid trends. So Esther was taken into the care of the local authority at five months, and later was described as 'difficult' in the nursery, where she stayed till fostered out at two years and a half.

During the first months after Esther left the nursery the foster mother had to put up with every kind of trouble, and for us this means that the child had not yet given up hope. Among other things she would lie down and scream in the street. Gradually matters improved a little, but the symptoms returned when, five months after Esther had been fostered – that is, when she was nearly three years old – a six-months-old boy was accepted into the family. This boy was adopted and Esther was never adopted. Esther would not let her foster mother be called 'mummy' by the boy, nor would she allow anyone to refer to the mother as the boy's 'mummy'. She became very destructive, and then she turned round and became very protective of the baby boy. The change came when the foster mother wisely allowed her to be a baby like the boy, treating her exactly as if she were six months old. Esther used this experience constructively, and started on her new career of being a mother. Along with this there developed a very good relationship with the foster father, which persisted. At the same time, however, the foster mother and Esther became more or less permanently at variance, so much so that, because of the rows between them, a psychiatrist advised that Esther, who was then five, should have a period away from home. Perhaps this was bad advice when we look back and see what was going on. The father, always sensitive to his daughter's needs, was instrumental in getting her home again. As he said, the whole of the child's belief in her foster home had gone dead. The man seems to have become this child's mother; and perhaps to this source can be traced the paranoid illness which he later developed, and his delusional system in which his wife appeared in the role of witch.

Esther steadily developed in spite of the great strain that was always present in the relationship between the two foster parents, who have since parted, and between whom there has arisen a perpetual legal feud. There is also the fact that the mother always openly preferred the adopted boy, and he has developed well enough to reward her in a straightforward way with his love.

This, then, is the sad and complicated story, in brief, of the authoress of the poem which seems to me to breathe security and home life. Let us follow up some of the implications of the case.

A very ill mother like Esther's real mother may have given her baby an exceptionally good start; this is not at all impossible. I think Esther's mother not only gave her a satisfactory breast-feeding experience, but also that ego support which babies need in the earliest stages, and which can be given only if the mother is identified with her baby. This mother was probably merged in with her baby to a high degree. My guess would be that she wanted to rid herself of her baby that she had been merged in with, that she had been at one with, because she saw looming up in front of her a new phase, which she would not be able to manage, a phase in which the infant would need to become separate from her. She would not be able to follow the baby's needs in this new stage of development. She could throw her baby away but she could not separate herself from the baby. Very deep forces would be at work at such a moment, and when the woman threw the baby into the canal (first choosing a time and place that made it almost certain that the baby would be rescued), she was trying to deal with some powerful unconscious conflict; such as, for example, her fear of an impulse to eat her child at the moment of separation from her. Be this as it may, the five-months-old baby may have lost at that moment of being thrown into the canal an ideal mother, a mother who had not yet become bitten, repudiated, pushed out, cracked open, stolen from, hated, as well as destructively loved; in fact an ideal mother to be preserved in idealization.

Then followed a long period of which we do not know the details, except that in the nursery to which the child was sent she remained difficult, that is to say, she retained something of the first good experience. She did not pass over into a compliant state, which would have meant that she had given up hope. By the time the foster mother came along a very great deal had happened. Naturally, as the foster mother began to mean something, Esther began to use the foster mother for the things that she had missed: biting, repudiating, pushing out, cracking open, stealing, hating. At this moment, surely, the foster mother needed, badly needed, someone to tell her what she was in for, what to expect, what to prepare herself for. Perhaps an attempt was made to let the foster mother know what was happening, but we have no record to tell us. She took over the child who had lost an ideal mother, and who had had a muddled experience from five months to two and a half years, and of course she took over a child with whom she had not the fundamental bond derived from early infant care. She did not in fact ever achieve a good relationship with Esther, although she easily managed the baby boy; and when later she fostered another girl, a third child, she repeatedly said to Esther: 'Now *this* is the child that I have always wanted.'

71

It was the father who was the good or idealized mother in Esther's life, and this lasted until the family broke up. Perhaps it was just this that split up the family, the father becoming more and more compelled to supply the mothering which this child needed, and the foster mother being forced more and more into the role of a persecutor in the child's life. This problem spoiled the otherwise satisfactory existence of the foster mother, who was doing well with her adopted son and her second fostered girl.

Esther has evidently inherited some of her mother's joy in words, and her mother's intelligence, and I think no one would say that she is in any way psychotic. Nevertheless, she suffers from a deprivation, one of her problems being a compulsion to steal. She also presents scholastic problems. She lives with the foster mother, who has become very possessive of her and has made access by the father almost impossible; and along with this the father has become awkward and has developed a serious psychiatric illness of a paranoid delusional nature.

The foster parents knew that Esther's mother was psychotic, that is to say that she was a certified patient, but they were not told the details, because the psychiatric social worker at the time recognized that these parents feared that Esther would inherit insanity. It is interesting that the worry about the inheritance of insanity in such cases seems to overlay the much more serious problem of the effect on the child of the period in the residential nursery before the fostering starts. During this period in Esther's case there was undoubtedly, from the child's point of view, a muddle, just where there ought to have been something very straightforward and simple, and indeed personal.

PSYCHOTIC ILLNESS

Parental psychosis does not produce childhood psychosis. Aetiology is not as simple as all that. Psychosis is not directly transmitted like dark hair or haemophilia, nor is it passed on to a baby by the nursing mother in her milk. It is not a disease. For those psychiatrists who are interested not so much in people as in diseases – diseases of the mind, they would call them – life is relatively easy. But for those of us who tend to think of psychiatric patients not as so many diseases but as people who are casualties in the human struggle for development for adaptation, and for living, our task is rendered infinitely complex. When we see a psychotic patient we feel 'here but for the grace of God go I'. We know the disorder, of which we see an exaggerated example.

Some sort of classification may help to distinguish the various types of illness. First, we can divide psychotic parents into fathers and mothers, for there are certain effects which concern only the mother-infant relationship, because this starts so early; or, if they concern the father, they concern him in his role of mother-substitute. It may be noted here that there is another role for a father, a more important one, in which he makes human something in the mother, and draws away from her the element which otherwise becomes magical and potent and spoils the mother's motherliness. Fathers have their own illnesses, and the effect of these on the children can be studied, but naturally, such illnesses do not impinge on the child's life in earliest infancy, and first the infant must be old enough to recognize the father as a man.

Then I would roughly divide the psychoses clinically into the manic-depressive psychoses, and the schizoid disorders which go right up to and include schizophrenia itself. Along with these disorders is a variable amount of delusion of persecution, either that which alternates with hypochondria or that which appears as a general paranoid over-sensitivity.

Let us now take schizophrenia, the most severe illness, and work towards clinical health (leaving out psychoneurosis, which does not concern us here).

If we look at the characteristics of schizoid persons, one thing we find is a weak delineation of the border between inner and external reality, between what is subjectively conceived of and what is objectively perceived. Then if we look we find feelings of unreality in the patient. Also schizoid persons merge in with people or things more easily than do normal people, and they experience more difficulty in feeling themselves to be separate. Further, we notice a relative failure on the part of schizoid people to become established on a body-ego basis; the psyche is not clearly linked with anatomy and the functioning of the body. The psyche-soma has a poor working relationship or partnership; perhaps the boundaries of the psyche do not exactly correspond with those of the body. On the other hand, the intellectual processes may run away with themselves. Schizoid men and women do not easily make relationships, nor do they maintain relationships well when they have made them with objects that are external to themselves, or real in the ordinary sense of the term. They make relationships on their own terms and not in terms of the impulses of other people.

Parents with these characteristics fail in many subtle ways in their handling of their infants (except in so far as they hand over their children to others, being aware of their own deficiency).

The Need to take a Child away from a Sick Parent

There is another point that I wish to make: in my practice I have always recognized the existence of a type of case in which it is essential to get a child away from a parent, especially a parent who is psychotic or severely neurotic. I could give many examples in illustration, of which I will describe briefly one, a girl, with severe anorexia:

This girl was eight years old when I removed her from her mother, and as soon as she got away she was found to be quite normal. The mother was in a state of depression, which on this occasion was reactive to the absence of her husband on war service. Whenever this mother became depressed the girl developed anorexia. Later, the mother had a boy, and in turn he developed the same symptom, in defence against her insane need to prove her value by stuffing food into her children. This time it was the daughter who brought her brother for treatment. I was unable to get the boy away from the mother even for a brief period, and he has not been able to establish himself as fully independent of his mother.

Often, in fact, we have to accept the fact that this or that child is caught up hopelessly in a parent's illness and nothing can be done about it. We have to recognize these cases in order to preserve our own sanity.

In various ways these psychotic characteristics in parents, and especially in mothers, do affect the development of the infant and child. It must be remembered, however, that *the child's illness belongs to the child*, although in the aetiology of the case environmental failure must be given full marks. A child may find some means of healthy growth in spite of environmental factors, or may be ill in spite of good care. When we arrange for a child to be cared for away from psychotic parents we expect to work with the child, and it is but seldom that we find that the child is normal when taken away from the ill parent, as in the case cited above.

The 'Chaotic' Mother

A very disturbing state in the mother, which seriously affects the children's lives, is the condition in which the mother is in a chaotic state – in fact, is in a state of organized chaos. This is a defence: a chaotic state of affairs has been set up and is steadily maintained, no doubt to hide a more serious underlying disintegration that constantly threatens. Mothers who are ill in this way are truly difficult to live with. Here is an example:

A woman patient who completed a long analysis with me had such a mother, and it may be that this is the most difficult kind of ill mother that one can have. The home looked like a good one, and the father was steady and benevolent, and there were many children. All the children were in one way or another affected by the mother's psychiatric state, which was very much like that of the mother's own mother.

This organized chaos compelled the mother constantly to break up everything into fragments, and to produce an infinite series of distractions in the children's lives. In all ways, and especially as soon as words could be used, this mother had continuously muddled my patient up, and never did anything else. She was not always bad; sometimes she was very good as a mother; but she always muddled everything up with distractions, and unpredictable and therefore traumatic actions. When talking to her child she employed puns and nonsense rhymes, jingles and half-truths, science fiction, and facts dressed up as imagination. The havoc she wrought was almost complete. Her children all came to grief, and the father was powerless and could only hide himself in his work.

Depressive Parents
Depression may be a chronic illness, giving a parent a poverty of available affect, or it may be a serious illness appearing in phases, with more or less sudden withdrawal of rapport. The depression that I am referring to here is not so much a schizoid depression as a reactive one. When an infant is at a stage of needing the mother to be preoccupied with infant care it can be severely disturbing to the infant suddenly to find the mother preoccupied with something else, something that simply belongs to the mother's own personal life. An infant in this position feels infinitely dropped. The following case shows the operation of this factor at a rather later stage, the child being two years old.

Tony had a strong obsession when he came to me at the age of seven. He was on the point of turning into a pervert with dangerous skills and he had already played at strangling his sister. This obsession was stopped when the mother talked to him, on my advice, about his feeling of losing her. This feeling had resulted from several early separations. The worst separation, and the significant one, was the mother's depression when the boy was two.

An acute phase in the mother's depressive illness cut her off from him most effectually, and any return of her depression in later years tended more than anything else to bring about a renewal of Tony's obsession with string. For him string is a last resort, joining together things which seem to be separated.[1]

So it was a melancholic phase in the chronic depression of an excellent mother in a good home that produced the deprivation which in turn evoked the presenting symptom in the case of Tony.

With some parents it is the manic-depressive mood swings which are a source of trouble for their children. It is amazing how even small children learn to gauge the parents' mood. They do this when each day starts, and sometimes they learn to keep an eye on the mother's or the father's face almost all the time. I suppose later on they look at the sky or listen to the weather forecast on the BBC.

As an example I give a boy of four years, a very sensitive boy, much like his father in temperament. He was in my consulting-room, playing on the

[1] See D. W. Winnicott, 'String', in *The Maturational Processes and the Facilitating Environment* (London: Hogarth Press, 1965).

75

floor with a train, while the mother and I talked about him. He suddenly said, without looking up: 'Dr Winnicott, are you tired?' I asked him what made him think so, and he said: 'Your face'; so he had evidently taken a good look at my face when he came into the room. Actually, I was very tired, but I had hoped to have hidden it. The mother said it was characteristic of him to gauge how people were feeling. because his father (an excellent father, a general practitioner) was a man who had to be nicely gauged before he could be used freely as a playmate. He was indeed often tired and rather depressed.

Children can deal, therefore, with mood swings in their parents by carefully observing them, but it is the unpredictability of some parents that can be traumatic. Once children have come through the earliest stages of maximal dependence, it seems to me that they can come to terms with almost any adverse factor that remains constant or that can be predicted. Naturally, children with high intelligence have an advantage over those with low intelligence in this matter of prediction, but sometimes we find that the intellectual powers of the highly intelligent children have been overstrained – the intelligence has been prostituted in the cause of predicting complex parental moods and tendencies.

Sick Parents as Therapists
Severe mental illness certainly does not prevent mothers or fathers from seeking help for their children at the right moment.

Percival, for instance, came to me in an acute psychotic episode when he was eleven. His father had had schizophrenia when twenty years old, and it was the father's psychiatrist who sent me the case. The father was now over fifty and he had come to terms with his chronic mental illness. He was acutely sympathetic with his son when he became ill. Percival's mother is herself a schizoid person, with a very poor reality sense; nevertheless, she was able to nurse her son through the early phase of his illness until he was well enough to be nursed and treated away from home. It took Percival three years to recover from his personal illness, which was very much bound up with the illness of both his parents.

I give this case because I was able to use both parents, although they were ill, or perhaps because they were ill, to see Percival through the first critical phase of his illness. The mother made herself into an excellent mental nurse and she allowed Percival's personality to merge in with hers exactly in the way that was needed. I knew she would not be able to do this for long, however, and after six months, when I got the SOS that I was expecting, I immediately placed Percival away from home, but the main job had been done.

The father's experience of schizophrenia enabled him to tolerate extreme madness in the boy, and the mother's condition made her participate in his illness until she began to need a new phase of mental nursing herself. Of course, as the boy got well one of the things he had to do was to learn that both his father and his mother were themselves ill, and he took this in his stride. He is now well on into puberty and, thanks very largely to his very ill parents, he is now healthy.

And what of this rather different story that comes from my hospital clinic?

The father in this family has cancer, not a psychiatric disorder. Doctors have miraculously kept him alive for ten years in spite of his cancer. The result is that his wife, the mother of many children, has not had a holiday for fifteen years, and she has absolutely given up hope. She just exists, and is completely taken up in the nursing of her bed-ridden husband and in the management of the home, which is dark, cramped, and depressing. She is full of guilt whenever anything goes wrong or when another child leaves home. One boy has become an alcoholic in adolescence. But the other children are doing well. The only happiness in the mother's life comes from her job, which she does from 6 to 8 in the morning. She pretends that she goes out to get some money, but she goes out for a change of scene, this being her only recreation. It seems to me that the father's cancer is a kind of joker which effectively disrupts the life of the whole family. Nothing can be done because cancer sits supreme at the head of the father's bed, grinning and omnipotent.

This is a terrible state of affairs; nevertheless, it would seem to me to be worse when one of the parents in a family, although physically healthy, has a psychiatric disorder of psychotic quality.

DEVELOPMENTAL STAGES AND PARENTAL PSYCHOSIS

In the theory behind these considerations one keeps in mind always the stage of development of the infant at the time of the operation of a traumatic factor. The infant may be almost entirely dependent, merged in with the mother, or may be ordinarily dependent and gradually gaining independence, or the child may have already become to some extent independent. In relation to these stages we may consider the effect of psychotic parents and we may grade the illnesses of the parents in the following rough way:

(a) Very ill parents. In this case others take over the care of the infants and the children.

(b) Less ill parents. There are periods during which others take over.

(c) Parents who have sufficient health to protect their children from their illness, and to ask for help.

(d) Parents whose illness includes the child, so that nothing can be done for the child without violating the rights a parent has over his or her child.

I for one do not want legal power to take children from parents except where cruelty or gross neglect awakens society's conscience. Nevertheless, I do know that decisions to take children from psychotic parents have to be made. Each case needs very careful examination, or in other words highly skilled casework.

10

Adolescence
Struggling through the Doldrums

There is at this present time a world-wide interest in adolescence and the problems of the adolescent. In almost all countries there are adolescent groups that make themselves evident in some way or other. Many studies of this phase of development are being made, and there has arisen a new literature, either of autobiography written by the young, or of novels that deal with the lives of teenage boys and girls. It is safe to assume that there is a connection between this development in our social awareness and the special social conditions of the times we live in.

One thing that must be recognized at the start by those who explore in this area of psychology is the fact that the adolescent boy or girl does not want to be understood. Adults must hide among themselves what they come to understand of adolescence. It would be absurd to write a book for adolescents on adolescence because this period of life is one which must be lived, and it is essentially a time of personal discovery. Each individual is engaged in a living experience, a problem of existing.

Cure for Adolescence
There exists one real cure for adolescence, and only one, and this cannot be of interest to the boy or girl who is in the throes. The cure for adolescence belongs to the passage of time and to the gradual maturation processes; these together do in the end result in the emergence of the adult person. This process cannot be hurried or slowed up, though indeed it can be broken into and destroyed, or it can wither up from within, in psychiatric illness.

We do sometimes need to remind ourselves that although adolescence is something that we have always with us, each adolescent boy or girl grows up in the course of a few years into an adult. Parents know this better than some sociologists do, and public irritation with the phenomenon of adolescence can easily be evoked by cheap journalism and by the public pronouncements of persons in key positions, with adolescence referred to as a problem, and the fact that each individual adolescent is in process of becoming a responsible society-minded adult left out of the argument.

79

There is a considerable measure of agreement among those concerned with dynamic psychology with regard to a general statement of adolescence in terms of the emotional development of the individual.

The boy or girl in this age-phase is dealing with his or her personal puberty changes. He or she comes to the developments in sexual capacity and to secondary sexual manifestations with a personal past history, and this includes a personal pattern in the organization of defences against anxiety o various kinds. In particular, *in health*, there has been in each individual an experience before the latency period of a full-blooded Oedipus complex, that is to say, of the two main positions in the triangular relationship with the two parents (or parent-substitutes); and there have been (in the experience of each adolescent) organized ways of warding off distress or of accepting and tolerating the conflicts inherent in these essentially complex conditions.

Also derived from the experiences of each adolescent's early infancy and childhood are certain inherited and acquired personal characteristics and tendencies, fixations to pregenital types of instinctual experience, residues of infantile dependence and of infantile ruthlessness; and further, there are all manner of illness patterns associated with failures of maturation at Oedipal and pre-Oedipal levels. Thus the boy or girl comes up to puberty with all patterns predetermined, because of infantile and early childhood experiences, and there is much that is unconscious, and much that is unknown because it has not yet been experienced.

There is room for a great deal of variation in individual cases as to the degree and type of the problem that may result, but the general problem is the same: How shall this ego organization meet the new id advance? How shall the pubertal changes be accommodated in the personality pattern that is specific to the boy or girl in question? How shall the adolescent boy or girl deal with the new power to destroy and even to kill, a power which did not complicate feelings of hatred at the toddler age? It is like putting new wine into old bottles.

The Environment
The part played by the environment is immensely significant at this stage, so much so that it is best, in a descriptive account, to assume the continued existence and interest of the child's own father and mother and of wider family organizations. Many of the difficulties of adolescents for which professional help is sought derive from environmental failure, and this fact only emphasizes the vital importance of the environment and of the family setting in the case of the vast majority of adolescents who do in fact achieve adult maturity, even if in the process they give their parents headaches.

Defiance and Dependence

A characteristic of the age group under examination is the rapid alternation between defiant independence and regressive dependence, even a coexistence of the two extremes at one moment of time.

The Isolation of the Individual

The adolescent is essentially an isolate. It is from a position of isolation that a beginning is made which may result in relationships between individuals, and eventually in socialization. In this respect the adolescent is repeating an essential phase of infancy, for the infant is an isolate, at least until he or she has repudiated the not-me, and has become set up as a separated-off individual, one that can form relationships with objects that are external to the self and outside the area of omnipotent control. It could be said that before the pleasure-pain principle has given way to the reality principle the child is isolated by the subjective nature of his or her environment.

Young adolescents are collections of isolates, attempting by various means to form an aggregate through the adoption of an identity of tastes. They can become grouped if they are attacked as a group, but this is a paranoid organization reactive to the attack; after the persecution the individuals return to their state of being an aggregate of isolates.

Sex Prior to Readiness for Sex

The sex experiences of younger adolescents are coloured by this phenomenon of isolation; and also by the fact that the boy or girl does not yet know whether he or she will be homosexual, heterosexual, or simply narcissistic. In many cases there is a long period of uncertainty as to whether a sex urge will turn up at all. Urgent masturbatory activity may be at this stage a repeated getting rid of sex, rather than a form of sex experience, and indeed compulsive heterosexual or homosexual activities may themselves at this age serve the purpose of a getting rid of sex or a discharge of tensions, rather than of a form of union between whole human beings. Union between whole human beings is more likely to appear, first, in aim-inhibited sex play, or in affectionate behaviour with the accent on sentiment. Here again is the personal pattern, waiting to join up with the instincts, but in the long meanwhile there has to be found some form of relief from sexual tension; and compulsive masturbation would be expected in a high proportion of cases, if we had an opportunity to know the facts. (A good motto for any investigator of the subject would be this: whoever asks questions must expect to be told lies.)

It is certainly possible to study the adolescent in terms of the ego coping with id changes, and the practising psycho-analyst must be prepared to meet this central theme, either manifest in the child's life or displayed cautiously in the material presented by the child in the analytic setting, or in the child's conscious and unconscious fantasy and in the deepest parts of the personal psychic or inner reality. Here, however, I will not pursue this approach, because my purpose is to survey adolescence in another way and to attempt to relate today's urgency of the adolescent theme to the social changes that belong to the past fifty years.

THE TIME FOR ADOLESCENCE

Is it not a sign of the health of a society that its teenagers are able to be adolescent at the right time, that is to say, at the age that covers pubertal growth? Among primitive peoples either the pubertal changes are hidden under taboos or else the adolescent is turned into an adult in the space of a few weeks or months by certain rites and ordeals. In our present society, adults are being formed by natural processes out of adolescents who move forward because of growth tendencies. This may easily mean that the new adults of today have strength and stability and maturity.

Naturally, there must be a price to pay for this. The many adolescent break-downs call for toleration and treatment; and also this new development puts a strain on society, for it is distressing for adults who have themselves been defrauded of adolescence to watch the boys and girls in a state of florid adolescence all round them.

THREE SOCIAL CHANGES

In my opinion there are three main social developments that have altered the whole climate for adolescents in adolescence:

(i) *Venereal disease* is no longer a bogy. The spirochaete and the gonococcus are no longer (as they were certainly felt to be fifty years ago) agents of a punishing God. Now they can be dealt with by penicillin and by appropriate antibiotics.[1]

(ii) *The development of contraceptive techniques* has given the adolescent the freedom to explore. This freedom is very new, the freedom to find out about sexuality and sensuality when there is not only an absence of a wish for parenthood, but also, as there nearly always is, a wish to avoid bringing into the world an unwanted and unparented baby. Of course, accidents happen

---

[1] I remember clearly a conversation with a girl, sometime after the first world war. She told me that it was only the fear of venereal disease that had kept her from being a prostitute. She was horrified at the idea I put forward in a simple conversation that venereal disease might one day be preventable or curable. She said that she could not imagine how she could have got through her adolescence (and she was only just coming through it) without this fear, which she had used in order to keep straight. She is now the mother of a large family and would be called a normal sort of person; but she had to come through her adolescent struggle and the challenge of her own instincts. She had a difficult time. She did a bit of thieving and lying, but she came through. But she held on to the venereal disease deterrent.

and will happen, and these accidents lead to unfortunate and dangerous abortions or to the birth of illegitimate children. But in examining the problem of adolescence we must accept the fact, I suggest, that the modern adolescent can explore, if he or she has a mind to, the whole area of sensuous living, without suffering the mental agony that accidental conception involves. This is only partly true because the mental agony associated with the fear of an accident remains, but the problem has been altered in the course of the last thirty years by this new factor. The mental agony now, we can see, comes from the individual child's innate guilt sense. I do not mean that every child has an innate guilt sense, but I mean that, in health, the child develops in a very complicated way a sense of right and wrong, a sense of guilt, and ideals, and an idea of what he or she wants for the future.

(iii) *The atom bomb* is perhaps producing even more profound changes than the two characteristics of our age that I have listed so far. The atom bomb affects the relationship between adult society and the adolescent tide, which seems to be for ever coming in. We have to carry on now on the basis that there *is not going to be another war*. Now it can be argued that there might be a war at any minute in some place in the world, but we know that we can no longer solve a social problem by organizing for a new war. So there is no longer any basis on which we can justify the provision of strong military or naval discipline for our children, however convenient it might be for us to be able to do so.

Here comes the effect of the atom bomb. If it no longer makes sense to deal with our difficult adolescents by preparing them to fight for their King and Country, then that is another reason why we are thrown back on the problem that there is this adolescence, a thing in itself. So now we have got to 'dig' adolescence.

The adolescent is pre-potent. In the imaginative life the potency of man is not just a matter of the active and passive of intercourse. It includes a man's victory over a man and a girl's admiration of the victor. All this now, I am suggesting, has to be wrapped up in the mystique of the café bar and in the occasional disturbance with knives. Adolescence has to contain itself much more than it has ever had to do before, and itself is pretty violent material – rather like the repressed unconscious of the individual, not so beautiful if opened out to the world.

When we think of the notorious atrocities of modern youth, we must weigh against them all the deaths that belong to the war that is not, and that is not going to be; against all the cruelty that belongs to the war that is not going to be; and against all the free sexuality that belongs to every war that has ever been but is not going to be again. So adolescence is here with us, which is evident, and it has come to stay.

These three changes are having an effect on our social concern, and this shows clearly in the way in which adolescence comes into prominence as something that is no longer to be hustled off the stage by false manoeuvres, like conscription.

THE UNACCEPTABILITY OF THE FALSE SOLUTION

It is a prime characteristic of adolescents that they do not accept false solutions. This fierce morality on the basis of the real and the false belongs also to infancy and to illness of schizophrenic type.

The cure for adolescence is the passage of time, a fact which has very little meaning for the adolescent. The adolescent looks for a cure that is immediate, but at the same time rejects one 'cure' after another because some false element in it is detected.

Once the adolescent can tolerate compromise, he or she may discover various ways in which the relentlessness of essential truths can be softened. For instance, there is a solution through identification with parent figures; or there can be a premature maturity in terms of sex; or there can be a shift of emphasis from sex to physical prowess in athletics, or from the bodily functions to intellectual attainment or achievement. In general, adolescents reject these helps, and instead they have to go through a sort of *doldrums area*, a phase, in which they feel futile and in which they have not yet found themselves. We have to watch this happening. But a total avoidance of these compromises, especially of the use of identifications and vicarious experience, means that each individual must start from scratch, ignoring all that has been worked out in the past history of our culture. Adolescents can be seen struggling to start again as if they had nothing they could take over from anyone. They can be seen to be forming groups on the basis of minor uniformities, and on the basis of some sort of group adherence which belongs to locality and to age. Young people can be seen searching for a form of identification which does not let them down in their struggle, *the struggle to feel real*, the struggle to establish a personal identity, not to fit into an assigned role, but to go through whatever has to be gone through. They do not know what they are going to become. They do not know where they are, and they are waiting. Because everything is in abeyance, they feel unreal, and this leads them to do certain things which feel real to them, and which are only too real in the sense that society is affected.

We do in fact get very much caught up with this curious thing about adolescents, *the mixture of defiance and dependence*. Those looking after adolescents will find themselves puzzled as to how boys and girls can be defiant to a degree and at the same time so dependent as to be childish, even infantile, showing patterns of the infantile dependence that dates from their earliest times. Moreover, parents find themselves paying out money to enable their children to be defiant against themselves. This is a good example of the way in which those who theorize and write and talk are operating in a layer that is different from the layer in which adolescents live, and in which parents or parent-substitutes are faced with urgent problems of management. The real thing here is not the theory but the impact of the one on the other, the adolescent and the parent.

ADOLESCENT NEEDS

So it is possible to gather together the needs that adolescents manifest:

The need to avoid the false solution.
The need to feel real or to tolerate not feeling at all.
The need to defy in a setting in which dependence is met and can be relied on to be met.
The need to prod society repeatedly so that society's antagonism is made manifest, and can be met with antagonism.

HEALTHY ADOLESCENCE AND ILLNESS PATTERNS

That which shows in the normal adolescent is related to that which shows in various kinds of ill person. For example:

The need to avoid the false solution corresponds with the psychotic patient's inability to compromise; compare also psychoneurotic ambivalence, and the deceptiveness and self-deception of health.
The need to feel real or not to feel at all is related to psychotic depression with depersonalization.
The need to defy corresponds with the antisocial tendency as it appears in delinquency.

From this it follows that in a group of adolescents the various tendencies tend to be represented by the more ill members of the group. For example, one member of a group takes an overdose of a drug, another lies in bed in a depression, another is free with the flick-knife. In each case the aggregate of isolates is grouped behind the ill individual, whose extreme symptom has impinged on society. Yet, for the majority of the individuals who are involved there is not enough drive behind the tendency to bring the symptom into inconvenient existence and to produce a social reaction.

The Doldrums
To repeat: if the adolescent is to get through this development stage by natural process, then there must be expected a phenomenon which could be

called *adolescent doldrums*. Society needs to include this as a permanent feature and to tolerate it, to react actively to it, in fact to come to meet it, *but not to cure it*. The question is, has our society the health to do this?

Complicating this issue is the fact that some individuals are too ill (with psychoneurosis or depression or schizophrenia) to reach a stage of emotional development that could be called adolescence, or they can reach it only in a highly distorted way. I have not included in this account a description of severe psychiatric illness as it appears at this age level; nevertheless, one type of illness cannot be set aside in any statement about adolescence, namely, delinquency.

Adolescence and the Antisocial Tendency

It is revealing to study the close relationship that exists between the normal difficulties of adolescence and the abnormality that may be called the antisocial tendency. The difference between these two states lies not so much in the clinical picture that each presents as in the dynamic, in the aetiology, of each. At the root of the antisocial tendency there is always a deprivation. It may simply be that the mother, at a critical time, was in a withdrawn state or depressed, or it may be that the family broke up. Even a minor deprivation, if it occurs at a difficult moment, may have a lasting result because it overstrains the available defences. Behind the antisocial tendency there is always some health and then an interruption, after which things were never the same again. The antisocial child is searching in some way or other, violently or gently, to get the world to acknowledge its debt; or is trying to make the world re-form the framework which got broken up. At the root, therefore, of the antisocial tendency there is this deprivation. At the root of adolescence in general it is not possible to say that there is inherently a deprivation, and yet there is something which is the same, but, being less in degree and diffused, it just avoids overstraining the available defences. So that in the group that the adolescent finds to identify with, or in the aggregate of isolates that forms into a group in relation to a persecution, the extreme members of the group are acting for the total group. All sorts of things in the adolescents' struggle – the stealing, the knives, the breaking out and the breaking in, and everything – all these have to be contained in the dynamic of this group, sitting round listening to jazz, or having a bottle party. And, *if nothing happens*, the individual members begin to feel unsure of the reality of their protest. and yet they are not in themselves disturbed enough to do the antisocial act which would make things right. But if in the group there is an antisocial member, or two or three, willing to do the antisocial thing which produces a social reaction, this makes all the others cohere, makes them feel real, and temporarily structures the group. Each individual member will be loyal and will support the one who will act for the group, although not one of them would have approved of the thing that the extreme antisocial character did.

I think that this principle applies to the use of other kinds of illness. The suicidal attempt of one of the members is very important to all the others. Or one of the group cannot get up; he is paralysed with depression, and has got a record-player playing very doleful music; he locks himself in his room and nobody can get near. The others all know that this is happening, and every now and again he comes out and they have a bottle party or something, and this may go on all night or for two or three days. Such happenings belong to the whole group, and the group is shifting and the individuals are changing their groups; but somehow the individual members of the group use the extremes to help themselves *to feel real*, in their struggle to get through this doldrums period.

It is all a problem of *how to be adolescent during adolescence*. This is an extremely brave thing for anybody to be, and some of these people are trying to achieve it. It does not mean that we grown-ups have to be saying: 'Look at these dear little adolescents having their adolescence; we must put up with everything and let our windows get broken.' That is not the point. The point is that we are challenged, and we meet the challenge as part of the function of adult living. But we meet the challenge rather than set out to cure what is essentially healthy.

The big challenge from the adolescent is to the bit of ourselves that has not really had its adolescence. This bit of ourselves makes us resent these people being able to have their phase of the doldrums, and makes us *want to find a solution for them*. There are hundreds of false solutions. Anything we say or do is wrong. We give support and we are wrong, we withdraw support and that is wrong too. We dare not be 'understanding'. But in the course of time we find that this adolescent boy and this adolescent girl have come out of the doldrums phase and are now able to begin identifying with society, with parents, and with all sorts of wider groups, without feeling threatened with personal extinction.

11

The Family and Emotional Maturity

The psychology with which I am concerned takes maturity to be synonymous with health. The child of ten who is healthy is mature for the child of ten; the healthy three-year-old is mature for the child of three; the adolescent is a mature adolescent and is not prematurely adult. The adult who is healthy is mature as an adult, and by this we mean that he or she has passed through all the immature stages, all the stages of maturity at the younger ages. The healthy adult has all the immaturities to fall back upon either for fun or in time of need, or in secret auto-erotic experience or in dreaming. To do justice to this concept of 'maturity at age' one would need to re-state the whole theory of emotional development, but I assume in my readers some knowledge of dynamic psychology and of the theory by which the psycho-analyst works.

Given this concept of maturity, then, my subject is the role of the family in the establishment of individual health. And this prompts the following question for consideration: can the individual achieve emotional maturity except in the setting of the family?

There are two ways of approaching the subject of individual development if we divide dynamic psychology into two parts. First there is the development of the instinctual life, the pregenital instinctual functions and fantasies building up into full sexuality, this being reached, as is well known, before the beginning of the latency period. Along this line of thought we arrive at the idea of adolescence at a time at which the puberty changes dominate the scene, and the defences against anxiety that were organized in the first years reappear or tend to reappear in the growing individual. All this is very familiar ground. By contrast, I want to take the other way of looking at things whereby each individual starts with almost absolute dependence, reaches to the lesser degrees of dependence, and so begins to achieve autonomy.

It may be profitable to think in this second way rather than in the first way. If we do so we need not be too much concerned with the age of a child or adolescent or adult. What we are concerned with is the environmental provision which is well adapted to the needs of the individual at any one particular moment. In other words, this is the same subject as that of maternal care, which changes according to the age of the infant, and which meets the early dependence of the infant and also the infant's reaching out towards independence. This second way of looking at life may be particularly suited to the study of healthy development, and our aim at the present moment is to study health.

Maternal care becomes parental care, the two parents together taking responsibility for their infant, and for the relationship between their infants and their children. Moreover, the parents are there to receive the 'contributing in' which comes from the healthy children in the family. Parental care evolves into the family, and the word family begins to extend itself further to include grandparents and cousins, and the people who become like relations because of their neighbourliness, or because they have some special significance – for instance, godparents.

When we examine this developing phenomenon, which starts with maternal care and goes right on to the persisting interest that the family has in the adolescent boy and girl, we cannot fail to be impressed by the human need for a steadily widening circle for the care of the individual, and also by the need the individual has for a place into which a contribution can be made from time to time when the individual has the urge to be creative, or to be generous. All these ever-widening circles are the mother's lap and her arms and her concern.

I have made much in my writings of the very delicate adaptation that mothers make to the needs of their infants, needs which vary from minute to minute. Who but the infant's mother troubles to know and feel the infant's needs? I should like to follow up this theme here and to say that it is only the child's own family that is likely to be able to continue this task started by the mother and continued by the mother and father, the task of meeting the individual's needs. These needs include dependence and the individual's striving towards independence. The task includes meeting the changing needs of the growing individual, not only in the sense of satisfying instincts, but also in the sense of being present to receive the contributing in that is a vital feature of human life. And this task further includes acceptance of the breaking out in defiance and also of the return to dependence that alternates with defiance.

Immediately it is evident that in referring to defiance and dependence I am discussing something which appears quite typically in adolescence and can be well observed there; in fact it constitutes a main problem of management: how to be there waiting when the adolescent becomes infantile and dependent, and takes everything for granted, and at the same time be able to meet the adolescent's need to strike out defiantly to establish a personal independence? It is likely to be the individual's own family that is best able and willing to meet such a claim, the simultaneous claim on the parents' tolerance of even violent defiance, and on their time, money and concern.

The adolescent who runs away has by no means lost the need for home and family, as is well known.

At this point I should like to recapitulate: the individual in the course of emotional growth is going from dependence to independence, and in health retains the capacity for shifting to and fro, from one to the other. This process is not achieved quietly and easily. It is complicated by the alternatives of defiance and of return from defiance to dependence. In defiance the individual breaks through whatever is immediately around him or her, giving security. In order that this breaking through shall be profitable, two things are necessary. The individual needs to find a wider circle ready to take over, and this is almost the same as saying that what is needed is the capacity to return to the situation that has been broken up. In a practical sense the little child needs to break away from the mother's arms and lap, but not to go into space; the breaking away has to be to a wider area of control; something that is symbolical of the lap from which the child has broken away. A slightly older child runs away from home, but at the bottom of the garden has finished running away. The garden fence is now symbolical of the narrower aspect of holding which has just been broken up, shall we say the house. Later, the child works out all these things in going to school and in relation to other groups that are outside the home. In each case these outside groups represent a getting away from the home, and yet at the same time they are symbolical of the home that has been broken away from and in fantasy broken up.

When these things go well, the child is able to come back home in spite of the defiance inherent in the going away. We would describe this in terms of the child's inner economy, in terms of the organization of the personal psychic reality. But to a large extent success in the discovery of a personal solution depends on the existence of the family and on the parental management. Put the other way round, it is very difficult for a child to work out the conflicts of loyalties in moving out and in without satisfactory family management. Understanding management is usually available because usually there is a family, and there exist parents who feel responsible and who like to take responsibility. In the vast majority of cases the home and the family do exist and do remain intact and do provide the individual with an opportunity for personal development in this important respect. A surprising number of people can look back and say that whatever mistakes were made their family *never really let them down*, any more than their mother let them down in the matter of maternal care during the first days, weeks, and months.

Within the home itself, when there are other children the individual child gains immeasurable relief from having opportunity for sharing problems. This is another big subject, but the point that I would make here is that when the family is intact and the brothers and sisters are true siblings, then each individual has the best opportunity for beginning to lead a social life. The main reason is that at the centre of everything is the relationship to the actual father and mother, and however much this separates the children because it makes them hate each other, its main effect is to bind them, and to create a situation in which it is safe to hate.

All this is only too easily taken for granted when there is an intact family, and we see the children growing up and presenting symptoms which are often symptoms of healthy development even though they are awkward and disturbing. It is when the family is not intact, or threatens to break, that we notice how important the intact family is. It is true that a threat of breakdown of the family structure does not necessarily lead to clinical illness in the children, because in some cases it leads to a premature emotional growth and to a precocious independence and sense of responsibility; but this is not what we are calling maturity at age, and it is not health, even if it has healthy features.

Let me enunciate a general principle. It would seem to me to be valuable to understand that as long as the family is intact then everything relates ultimately to the individual's actual father and mother. In the conscious life and fantasy the child may have got away from the father and mother, and may have gained great relief from doing so. Nevertheless, the way back to the father and mother is always retained in the unconscious. In the unconscious fantasy of the child it is always on his or her own father and mother that a claim is made fundamentally. The child gradually comes to lose much or nearly all of the direct claim on the actual father and mother, but this is conscious fantasy. What has happened is that gradually displacement has taken place from the actual parents outwards. The family exists as something which is cemented by this fact, that for each individual member of the family the actual father and mother are alive in the inner psychic reality.

In this way we see two tendencies. The first is the tendency in the individual to get away from the mother and away from the father and mother and away from the family, each step giving increased freedom of ideas and of functioning. The other tendency works in the opposite direction and it is the need to retain or to be able to regain the relationship with the actual father and mother. It is this second tendency which makes the first tendency a part of growth instead of a disruption of the individual's personality. It is not a question of recognizing intellectually that the ever-widening area of relationships retains symbolically the idea of the father and the mother. What I am referring to is the individual's ability actually to get back to the parents and to the mother, back to the centre or back to the beginning, at any appropriate moment, perhaps in the flash of a dream or in the form of a poem or in a joke. The origin of all the displacements is in the parents and in the mother, and this needs to be retained. This is something which has a wide area of application: we can think, for example, of the emigrant, who finds a way of life in the antipodes and eventually comes back to make sure that Piccadilly Circus is as it was. I hope by this to have shown that if the unconscious fantasy is taken into account, which of course it must be, the child's constant exploration of wider areas and the child's constant search for groups outside the family and the child's defiant destruction of all rigid forms are the same thing as the child's need to retain the primary relationship to the actual parents.

In the healthy development of the individual, at whatever stage, what is needed is a steady progression, that is to say, a well-graduated series of defiant iconoclastic actions, each in the series being compatible with the retention of an unconscious bond with the central figures or figure, the parents or the mother. If families are observed it will be seen that immense trouble is taken in the natural course of events by parents to maintain this series and to organize the graduation so that the sequence of the individual's development is not broken.

A special case is provided in the sexual development, both in the establishment of a personal sexual life and in the search for a mate. In marriage there is expected a coincidental breaking out and away from the actual parents and the family, and at the same time a carry-through of the idea of family-building.

In practice these violent episodes are often hidden by the process of identification, especially identification of the boy with the father and of the girl with the mother. A life solution in terms of identification is not satisfactory, however, except in so far as the individual boy or girl has reached the dream of violent overthrow. In relation to this theme of the repeated breakthrough which is characteristic of the lives of growing individuals, the Oedipus complex comes as a relief, since in the triangular situation the boy can retain the love of the mother with the idea of the father in the way, and similarly the girl with the mother in the way can retain the longing for the father. Where only the child and the mother are concerned, there are only two alternatives, to be swallowed up or to break free.

The more we examine these matters the more we see how difficult it is for any group to take all the trouble that is required to keep these things going well unless that group is the family to which the child belongs.

It is hardly necessary for me to add that the opposite cannot be assumed; that is to say, if the family does its best for a child in all these respects, this does not mean that the child will therefore develop to full maturity. There are many hazards in the internal economy of each individual, and personal psychotherapy is mainly directed towards the clearing up of these internal strains and stresses. To follow up this theme would be to go over to the other way of looking at individual growth that I referred to at the beginning of this section.

It is useful to remember, when considering the role of the family, the contributions that have been made by social psychology and anthropology on this subject. In regard to social psychology, Willmott and Young's recent study, *Family and Kinship in East London,*[1] may be mentioned. In regard to anthropology, we are familiar with the ways in which various aspects of the family vary from locality to locality and from time to time; how sometimes it is the uncles and aunts who bring up the children, and the actual paternity may be lost as far as consciousness is concerned, but there is always evidence of unconscious knowledge of true parenthood.

To return to the concept of maturity as health. It is only too easy for individuals to jump forward a stage or two, to become mature in advance of their age, to become very well established as individuals where they ought to be less well established and more dependent. It is necessary to keep this in mind when we study the emotional maturity or immaturity of individuals who have been brought up away from their own families. These individuals may develop in such a way that at first we feel like making the comment: how established and how independent he or she is, and what a good thing it must be to have to fend for oneself early in life! I do not accept this, however, as a final statement, because I feel that for maturity it is necessary the individuals shall not mature early, not become established as individuals when in their age group they should be relatively dependent.

When I now look back, and consider the question that I raised tentatively at the outset, my conclusion is that if one accepts the idea of health as maturity at age, the emotional maturity of the individual cannot be achieved except in a setting in which the family has provided the bridge leading out of parental care (or maternal care) right across into the social provision. And it must be remembered that social provision is very much an extension of the family. If we examine the ways in which people provide for young children and for older children, and if we look at the political institutions of adult life, we find displacements from the home setting and the family. We find, for instance, the provision of opportunity for children who break away from their own homes to find a home from which they can once more break away if necessary. The home and the family are still the models on which is based any sort of social provision which is likely to work.

There are two main features, then, which (in the language that I have chosen to use here) the family contributes to the emotional maturity of the individual: one is the continued existence of the opportunity for dependence of a high degree; the other is the provision of the opportunity for the individual to break away from the parents to the family, from the family to the social unit just outside the family, and from that social unit to another, and perhaps to another and another. These ever-widening circles, which eventually become political or religious or cultural groupings in society, and perhaps nationalism[2]

[1] Young, M., and Willmott, P. (1957). London: Routledge & Kegan Paul.
[2] However much we long for a grouping that is international, we cannot afford to slur over the idea of nationalism as a stage in development.

itself, are the end-product of something that starts off with maternal care, or parental care, and then continues as the family. It is the family that seems to be especially designed to carry the unconscious dependence on the father and mother, the actual father and mother, and this dependence covers the growing child's need defiantly to break out.

This way of reasoning uses the concept of adult maturity equated with psychiatric health. It could be said that the mature adult is able to identify himself or herself with environmental groupings or institutions, and to do so without loss of a sense of personal going-on-being, and without too great a sacrifice of spontaneous impulse, this being at the root of creativity. If we examined the area covered by the term 'environmental groupings', then the highest marks would go to the widest meaning of the term, and to the most comprehensive area of society with which the individual feels identified. An important feature is the individual's capacity, after each example of icono-clastic acting out, to rediscover in the broken-up forms the original maternal care and parental provision and family stability, all of that on which the individual was dependent in the early stages. It is the family's function to pro-vide a practice ground for this essnetial feature of personal growth.

Here two sayings come surprisingly together:

(i) Things aint wot they was!
(ii) *Plus ça change, plus c'est la même chose.*

Mature adults bring vitality to that which is ancient, old, and orthodox by re-creating it after destroying it. And so the parents move up a step, and move down a step, and become grandparents.

Part 2

12

Theoretical Statement of the Field of Child Psychiatry

I. THE PROFESSIONAL FIELD

It is only now becoming understood that the half of paediatrics which is psychology is as big as the other half which concerns the tissues and the effect on the body and body functions of physical disease. Paediatrics is based on *a priori* knowledge of physical growth, and of disorders of body growth and body functioning. Psychiatry is based on an understanding of the emotional growth of the normal infant, child, adolescent, and adult, and of the developing relationship of the individual to external reality.

The place of academic psychology needs to be considered here. It stands at the borderline between physical growth and emotional growth. The academic psychologist studies manifestations which, although they are psychological, do in fact belong to physical growth. An example would be the skills that develop *pari passu* with brain growth and with the development of coordination, or the skills that do not develop because of physical brain lesions. In illustration it can be said: the academic psychologist is interested in the age at which a child can walk; dynamic psychology must take into account, however, the fact that one child may be driven by anxiety to walk earlier than the natural time, or may be delayed in walking by emotional factors. It would seldom happen that the date at which a child first walks would indicate exactly the capacity to walk based on physiological and anatomical growth.

The important subject of intelligence-testing also illustrates the academic psychologist's concern with a child's capacity that is based on the quality of the brain as a functioning organ. The academic psychologist is interested in any method which eliminates the emotional factors that disturb the 'pure' result of a test. When the clinician is using the intelligence-test rdsult, he must reclothe what he is given with the dynamic psychology which has been deliberately stripped off. A psychiatric interview is essentially different from a test interview; the two cannot be mixed. It is even difficult for one individual

97

help the woman to get to the true source of her guilt sense – as might be done in a psycho-analytic treatment of several years. What we can do is to give a little help over a period of time *at the exact place that the individual reports failure, and in so doing communicates hope.*

The main point that I wish to make is that when a mother's depression expresses itself in terms of a worry or a muddle we have a way of treating the depression – we can tackle this worry or muddle. We shall *not usually clear up the depression* by this means, and often the best we can do is to break up a vicious circle in which the muddle or a neglect of children is feeding back and reinforcing the depression. For our own sanity we must know that it is the depression that is the trouble and not the presenting worry. Often we watch the depression lift, and we then see the mother able to manage the details which for many weeks or even months have defeated her. Or she begins to get back the help of friends.

And as the depression lifts the woman will tell us that it was all due to constipation which she treated by taking herbs recommended by the grocer's wife. We shall not mind. We know we have played a part, indirectly affecting the woman's illness and strengthening her power to resolve her inner struggle that was so fully engaging her in the unconscious.

CLINICAL EXAMPLES

A girl comes to me for analytic treatment. I shall not refer to the long-term analysis of her liability to depression. She is now out of the mental hospital where she was for one year, and she is back at work and liable to recurring short depression phases.

Recently she came depressed. It was all about the heating for her new flat. She had tried to save money by mending the old fitting and now she was faced with buying a new one. How could she ever earn enough to live? She could see no future for herself – only a losing battle, and a solitary life. She sobbed all the session.

When she got home she found that her heating problem had been solved, and also that someone had sent her some money. The important thing for us, though, is that her depression lifted on her way home, before she found the gift heater and the money. By the time these welcome gifts came she was full of hope, and though no change had occurred in her actual position in the world she had but little doubt that she could earn a living, and I had shared her phase of hopelessness.

I suggest that our work becomes intelligible as well as rewarding if we keep in mind the heavy weight of depression which has to resolve itself inside the depressed person, while we try to help with whatever happens to be the imto be easy in both roles, that of psychologist doing a test and that of psychiatrist.

In fact, the psychiatrist makes particular use of that which the psychologist tries to eliminate, the emotional complexity. The psychiatrist's aim is not to make a test, but to become involved in the pattern of the patient's emotional life, to feel what it is like to so involved, and so to know rather than to know about the patient.

The social worker is in the same position in these matters as the psychiatrist.

Academic psychology appears at first sight to be more scientific than dynamic psychology. Both in clinical medicine and in psychiatry there are those who work better in a laboratory. It is a fact, however, that human beings are made up of feelings and feeling patterns, and to know the mind's shape is not to know the person's psyche. Clinical problems in child psychiatry largely concern the psyche, the personality, the person, and the inner and external life of feeling.[1]

Doctor as Adviser

It often happens that a doctor finds himself in a false position because, being an authority in physical medicine, he is expected to be an authority in psychology. Emotional illness he may recognize, and so refer the matter to a psychiatric colleague. When he is expected to know about normal emotional development, however, he is likely to get out of his depth. He is not trained to give advice to parents with regard to the nurture of a normal child. He may of course draw on his own experience as a parent, but psychology cannot be learned by parents watching their own infants and themselves.

The study of the emotional development of the infant, and of parental care and child care in general, is in fact a scientific discipline and a highly complex one, which makes great demands on the student. It is not a matter of 'being good with children'; it is quite a different thing. It could be added that if parents have succeeded as parents they are unaware of the things in themselves that have made for success. It could almost be said that they are better equipped to give advice about child care if they have failed than if they have succeeded, because the very failure may have led them to examine the subject of child care in an objective manner.

Obviously, the paediatrician who is thoroughly at home on the physical side of child care cannot just slip over to child psychiatry. Effort is neded, a new science has to be met, and gradually a new skill has to be built up, based on a science which is not included in the curriculum of the medical student. If this is true of the paediatrician it is also true of the teacher and of the social worker.

---

[1] This having been said, it must be insisted that the author is not belittling the part played by academic psychology.

Psychosomatic Dichotomy

Nowhere is the need for an understanding of these matters more clear than in the treatment of the psychosomatic disorders. In practice it is very difficult to find a physically-minded paediatrician who cooperates easily and on equal terms with a psycho-analytically-orientated psychotherapist, each believing in the other's integrity, and each knowing of the other's work. In practice the child is torn not only internally between the factors that tend towards physical and those that tend towards psychological manifestations, but also externally by the tug-of-war between the doctors. The child who needs hospitalization for a psychosomatic disorder either goes into a hospital ward and so becomes the responsibility of a physically-minded paediatrician; or else enters an institution such as an adult mental hospital, or a hostel which specializes in the management of difficult children, with the result that the paediatrician is no longer in touch with events.

There do exist outpatient clinics which a child may attend over a long period of time without being labelled a physical or a psychiatric case. These provide the only good type of background for the practice of psychosomatic medicine.

PAEDIATRICS AND CHILD PSYCHIATRY

The development of the relationship between paediatrics and child psychiatry can be presented in the following terms. The paediatrician, expecting to be fully occupied in the study of physical disease, prepares himself by study of the physical sciences. Paediatrics draws to itself those to whom the physical sciences make an appeal. Out of paediatrics there eventually emerges a study of the healthy body. Paediatrics makes its specific contribution through being involved in the problem of growth. Gradually the physical studies lead the paediatrician to an understanding of the infant's bodily needs at a stage of full physical dependence.

In paediatrics there is a tendency towards the use of the laboratory in the place of the clinic. The ward almost becomes a laboratory. The outpatient clinic tends to be brought into line with the conditions of the ward.

The study of the healthy child, however, involves the paediatrician more and more in the provision of conditions for that study which are near to those that are natural to the child and far removed from the controlled conditions of a laboratory. The clinician cannot do his work without a natural understanding of and sympathy with the child as a person, and he necessarily becomes involved with the child's use of the environment during growth, and with all the problems of nurture. Thus the paediatrician who is a clinician veers towards psychiatry and finds himself in the position of adviser in child care, although in fact he is not especially equipped to fulfil this role.

The end of the second world war found paediatrics in Great Britain physically orientated, and with tremendous achievements to its credit on the physical side. As a result of these achievements the quantity of physical disease had already diminished, and a further steady decrease in physical disease could be predicted to follow the spread of paediatric services over the whole country.

By this time, too, a very great deal of work had been done on the normal emotional development of infants and of children of various ages, and on psychopathology also; furthermore, the training of psycho-analysts and child analysts had become organized. It was Freud who, many years previously, had shown that in the treatment of adult neurotic disturbances the analyst constantly reaches to the child or to the infant in the adult; and the implication of this was that eventually it would be possible to do preventive work directly with the child and even with the infant, and in the realm of child care. As has been proved, it has also become possible to treat the psychiatric child case with the child still a child and still in a dependent state. There is now an increasing tendency for paediatrics to be concerned both with the *physical* side of development and with *emotional* development, along with which goes the development of the human personality and of the relationship of the child to the family and to the social environment.

PSYCHO-ANALYSIS AND THE CHILD

There has been an evolution, too, in the psycho-analyst's orientation to the child. This evolution could perhaps be described in the following way. The practising psycho-analyst is treating all kinds of adult patients, those who pass for *normal*, those who are *neurotic*, those who are *antisocial*, and those who are on the borderline of *psychotic*. In all cases, while he is also concerned with the present-day problems of the patient, he finds that his main work draws him to a study of the childhood, and even the infancy, of the patient. The next step therefore in his experience is for him to treat adolescents, and children, and small children, and to become involved in the emotional life of the actual child rather than of the child in the adult. He conducts child analyses, takes part in the management of child-psychiatry cases, and discusses infant care with parents. In doing psychotherapy the psycho-analyst is in a strong position to study the whole child. Disturbances of physical health due to emotional disorder thus come naturally into the analyst's province, as also do emotional distortions that are secondary to physical illness. Physical illness, however, demands the knowledge acquired in the course of the past century by the physically-orientated paediatrician.

The psycho-analyst needs to be reminded that the physical health which he takes for granted depends on the preventive aspect of physical paediatrics, and also on midwifery, which has very much reduced infant mortality in recent decades and has made childbirth relatively safe.

But who shall have concern for the whole child?

II. THE CHILD PATIENT

ASPECTS OF THE PSYCHIATRIC PROBLEM STUDIED IN SEQUENCE

Let us now consider the problem that confronts anyone who becomes involved with a child in the therapeutic situation. There are three sets of phenomena, each interrelated, but nevertheless distinct for descriptive purposes. (In this description, physical health is taken for granted.)

(i) The Normal Difficulties of Life

Normality or health is a matter of maturity, not a matter of freedom from symptoms. The normal child of four years, for instance, experiences very severe anxiety simply on account of the fact that there are conflicts in human relationships inherently associated with life and living and with the management of instincts. It is a paradox that at certain ages – as, for instance, at four years – a normal child may display the full range of symptomatology (frank anxiety, temper tantrums, phobias, obsessional compulsions, disturbances in the related physical functioning, dramatizing, conflict in the emotional sphere, etc.) whereas, on the other hand, an almost symptom-free child may be severely ill. Naturally the experienced psychiatrist can see through this façade, but from the point of view of the untrained observer, which description may easily include the physically-orientated paediatrician, the ill child may seem more normal.

(ii) The Childhood Neurosis (or Psychosis) that is Manifest

At the various ages from infancy to adulthood there is to be found psychiatric illness. Defence organizations against intolerable anxiety produce a symptomatology that may be recognized, diagnosed, and often treated. In some cases the environment is normal enough, in others an external factor is aetiologically significant.

(iii) Latent Neurosis or Psychosis

The psychiatrist learns, further, to see in the child the potential illness, that which may appear later under stress, stress of trauma or stress of adolescence, or of adulthood and independence. This third task of the child psychiatrist is very difficult but not impossible. As an example, we can take the rather common phenomenon of an organized false self. A false self may fit in well with the family pattern, or perhaps with an illness in the mother, and it can very easily be mistaken for health. Yet it implies instability and a liability to breakdown.

These three aspects of psychiatric disorder in a child, though interrelated, are distinct in any theoretical formulation of the emotional development of the human being.

HEALTH AS EMOTIONAL MATURITY

The psychiatrist is concerned with development, the emotional development of the individual. In psychiatry ill health and immaturity are almost synonymous. Treatment, from the psycho-analyst's point of view, aims at enabling maturity to arrive even at a late date. The teaching of child psychiatry is therefore based on instruction in child development. Academic psychology is an important adjunct to the general study of emotional development. Emotional development starts at an early date, round about the birth date, and leads towards the mature adult. The adult who is mature is able to identify with the environment, and to take part in the establishment, maintenance, and alteration of the environment, and to make this identification without serious sacrifice of personal impulse.

What precedes adult maturity? The answer to this question covers the whole of the vast subject of child psychiatry. I have attempted below a brief statement of the psychology of the child by the method chosen, starting at the end and working backwards to earliest infancy.

Adult Maturity
World citizenship represents an immense and rare achievement in the development of the individual, scarcely compatible with personal health or with freedom from the depressed mood. Apart from isolated examples, mature adults enjoy health on the basis of membership of a group within the total group, and the more limited the size of the group the less apposite is the epithet mature. Thus there can be seen those who achieve health but in a limited group, and those who strive for the wider group and suffer ill health.

Adolescence
Adolescence is characterized as much as anything else by society's limited expectation of the adolescent, who is not expected to have reached full socialization. In fact, for adolescents we provide self-limited groups, and the hope is that the individual adolescent will be able to make use of the graduated extension of the size and scope of the group that demands loyalty. The adolescent displays a mixture of defiant independence and dependence. The two states alternate or even coexist. In this way adolescence presents a paradox. It will be seen that each of these extremes takes adult control for

granted, and therefore groups designed for adolescents must to some extent have adult backing.

Latency

The human child at the age of five or six enters a period known in psychology as the latency period, in which the biological drive behind the instinctual life is modified. It is in this period that the main work of the teacher is done, since in health the child is for the time being relatively uninvolved in emotional *growth* and instinct *change*.

There are certain characteristics of the latency period: the tendency of boys towards hero-worship, and towards the gang or an association with other boys on the basis of some quest; personal friendships do exist, however, and may cut across the ever-changing gang loyalties. In girls there are similar features, especially when girls have, as they well may have at this stage, boyish interests. As girls they have some capacity for enjoying being like mother, in the house, in the management of other children, and in the mysteries of shopping.

First Maturity

In the stage before the latency period the child, in health, reached the full capacity for the adult dream or game, with the appropriate instincts and with the resultant anxieties and conflicts. This capacity can be attained only in a family setting that is relatively stable. In this period, from roughly two to five years of age, a tremendous quantity of life is lived. It is telescoped into a short period of time by adult standards, but it is doubtful whether the whole of the rest of life is as long as these three years, in which the child has become a whole person, living among whole people, loving and hating, and dreaming and playing.

In this period the child may be expected to display every possible kind of symptom, that is to say, characteristics that must be called symptoms if they persist or are exaggerated. The key to this period, which is the time at which neurosis takes its origin, is anxiety, and by anxiety here is meant a very severe experience, of the kind which appears clinically in the nightmare. Anxiety concerns the conflict, largely in the unconscious, between love and hate. The various symptoms are either overflows of anxiety or else the beginnings of organizations that are aimed at defending against anxiety that is intolerable. Neurosis is no more nor less than a rigidity in the organization of defence against anxiety that arises out of the instinctual life of the child at this age. This is true of neurosis at whatever age it becomes apparent.

There is a very complex psychology of this period, much of which is now understood, and this understanding was not possible until Freud initiated scientific examination of the affairs of the small child, which he did largely during the treatment of adults. It is here that Freud's insistence on infantile sexuality, by which is meant the instinctual life that is central to the child of this age, at first made psycho-analysis unpopular, although it can now be said that the main principles enunciated by Freud are accepted. The difficulty now is in the matter of understanding the tremendous forces that are at work, and that underlie both the symptomatology of this period and also emotional health, which may be attained by the time a child is five years old and entering into the latency period.

Infancy

Prior to this stage to which reference has been made, in which the child is essentially involved in triangular relationships, there is the stage at which the child is involved only with the mother, and yet as a whole human being with another whole person. It is somewhat artificial to draw a line between this earlier stage and that of the child's involvement in the triangular situation; but the former is an important stage, and the anxieties belonging to it are of a different order. Thdy concern ambivalence, that is to say, love and hate directed towards the same object. The psychiatric condition related to this stage is more of the nature of affective disorder, depression, paranoia, and less of the order of neurosis.

Earliest Infancy

Earlier still, the infant is in a highly dependent state and is engaged in certain essential preliminary tasks, such as the integration of the personality into a unit, the indwelling of the psyche in the body, and the initiation of contact with external reality. The dependent state of the infant is such that these early tasks cannot be performed without good-enough mothering. Illness derived from this early stage is of the nature of psychosis, that is to say, one or other of the disturbances described under the word schizophrenia.

Here is the place where research is now active. Much is uncertain and is under discussion, but out of what is known it appears to be true that mental health is laid down at the beginning, during this stage in which the infant is dependent to a high degree on the capacity of the mother or the mother-substitute to adapt to the infant's needs, a feat which she manages only by an identification with the infant that arises out of her attitude of devotion.

CONCLUSION

In thus tracing back the psychology of the child we pass from the individual's ability to take part in the creation, maintenance, and alteration of the environment to the state of absolute dependence which belongs to the beginning. In the course of progress from the latter to the former the infant makes a very complex personal development, which in spite of its complexity can now be outlined and to some extent accurately described.

The field of child psychiatry covers the state of the whole child, along with the child's past and the child's potential for health of mind and richness of adult personality. The child psychiatrist is mindful of the fact that in the individual child's emotional development is contained society's potential for family functioning and for the institution and maintenance of social groupings.

13

The Contribution of Psycho-Analysis to Midwifery

It should be remembered that it is the midwife's skill, based on a scientific knowledge of the physical phenomena, that gives her patients the confidence in her that they need. Without this basic skill on the physical side she may study psychology in vain, because she will not be able to substitute psychological insight for knowing what to do when a placenta praevia complicates the birth process. However, given the requisite knowledge and skill, there is no doubt that the midwife can add greatly to her value by acquiring also an understanding of her patient as a human being.

PLACE OF PSYCHO-ANALYSIS

How does psycho-analysis come into the subject of midwifery? In the first place, through its minute study of detail in long and arduous treatments of individual people. Psycho-analysis is beginning to throw light on all sorts of abnormality such as menorrhagia, repeated abortion, morning sickness, primary uterine inertia; and many other physical states can sometimes have as part of their cause a conflict in the unconscious emotional life of the patient. Much has been written about these psychosomatic disorders. Here, however, I am concerned with another aspect of the psycho-analytic contribution: I will try to indicate, in general terms, the effect of psycho-analytic theories on the relationships between the doctor, the nurse, and the patient, with reference to the situation of childbirth.

Psycho-analysis has already led to a very big change in emphasis which shows itself in the attitude of midwives today compared with those of twenty years ago. It is now accepted that the midwife wants to add to her essential basic skill some assessment of the patient as a person – a person who was born, was once an infant, has played at mothers and fathers, has been scared of the developments that come at puberty, has experimented with new-found adolescent urges, has taken the plunge and has married (perhaps), and has either by design or by accident fallen with child.

If the patient is in hospital she is concerned about the home to which she will return, and in any case there is the change which the birth of the baby will make to her personal life, to her relationship with her husband, and to the parents of both herself and her husband. Often, also, complications are to be expected in her relationship to her other children, and in the feelings of the children towards each other.

If we all become persons in our work, then the work becomes much more interesting and rewarding. We have, in this situation, four persons to consider, and four points of view. First there is *the woman*, who is in a very special state which is like an illness, except that it is normal. *The father*, to some extent, is in a similar state, and if he is left out the result is a great impoverishment. *The infant* at birth is already a person, and there is all the difference between good and bad management from the infant's point of view. And then *the midwife*. She is not only a technician, she is also human; she has feelings and moods, excitements and disappointments; perhaps she would like to be the mother, or the baby, or the father, or all in turn. Usually she is pleased and sometimes she feels frustrated to be the midwife.

Essentially Natural Process

One general idea goes right through what I have to say: that is, that there are natural processes which underlie all that is taking place; and we do good work as doctors and nurses only if we respect and facilitate these natural processes.

Mothers had babies for thousands of years before midwives appeared on the scene, and it is likely that midwives first came to deal with superstition. The modern way of dealing with superstition is the adoption of a scientific attitude; science being based on objective observation. Modern training, based on science, equips the midwife to ward off superstitious practices. What about fathers? Fathers had a definite function before doctors and the welfare state took it over: they not only felt themselves the feelings of their women, and went through some of the agony, but also they took part, warding off external and unpredictable impingements, and enabling the mother to become preoccupied, to have but one concern, the care of the baby that is there in her body or in her arms.

Change in Attitude to the Infant

There has been an evolution of attitude with regard to the infant. I suppose that throughout the ages parents have assumed that the infant was a person, seeing in the infant much more than was there – a little man or woman. Science at first rejected this, pointing out that the infant is not just a little adult, and for a long time infants were regarded by objective observers as scarcely human till they started to talk. Recently, however, it has been found that infants are indeed human, though appropriately infantile. Psycho-analysis has been gradually showing that even the birth process is not lost on the infant, and that there can be a normal or an abnormal birth from the infant's point of view. Possibly every detail of the birth (as felt by the infant) is recorded in the infant's mind, and normally this shows in the pleasure that people get in games that symbolize the various phenomena that the infant experienced – turning over, falling, sensations belonging to the change from being bathed in fluid to being on dry land, from being at one temperature to being forced to adjust to temperature change, from being supplied by pipeline to being dependent for air and food on personal effort.

THE HEALTHY MOTHER

One of the difficulties that is encountered with regard to the midwife's attitude to the mother ranges round the problem of diagnosis. (Here I do not mean the diagnosis of the bodily state, which must be left to the nurse and the doctor, nor will I refer to bodily abnormality; I am concerned with the healthy and the unhealthy in the psychiatric sense.) Let us start with the normal end of the problem.

At the healthy extreme the patient is not a patient, but is a perfectly healthy and mature person, quite capable of making her own decisions on major matters, and perhaps more grown-up than the midwife who attends her. She happens to be in a dependent state because of her condition. Temporarily she puts herself in the nurse's hands, and to be able to do that in itself implies health and maturity. In this case the nurse respects the mother's independence for as long as possible, and even throughout the labour if the confinement is easy and normal. In the same way, she accepts the complete dependency of the many mothers who can go through the experience of childbirth only by handing over all control to the person in attendance.

Relationship of Mother, Doctor, and Nurse

I suggest that it is because the healthy mother is mature or adult that she cannot hand over the controls to a nurse and a doctor whom she does not know. She gets to know them first, and this is the important thing of the period leading up to the time of the confinement. She either trusts them, in which case she will forgive them even if they make a mistake; or else she does not trust them, in which case the whole experience is spoiled for her; she fears to hand over, and attempts to manage herself, or actually fears her condition; and she will blame them for whatever goes wrong whether it is their fault or not. And rightly so, if they failed to let her get to know them.

I put first and foremost this matter of the mother and the doctor and nurse getting to know each other, and of continuity of contact, if possible, throughout the pregnancy. If this cannot be achieved, then at least there must be a very definite contact with the person who is to attend the actual confinement, well before the expected date of the confinement.

A hospital set-up which does not make it possible for a woman to know in advance who will be her doctor and her nurse at the time of the confinement is no good, even if it be the most modern, well-equipped, sterile, chromium-plated clinic in the country. It is this sort of thing that makes mothers decide to have their babies at home, with the family practitioner in charge, and with hospital facilities available only in case of serious emergency. I personally think that mothers should be fully supported in their idea when they want a home confinement, and that it would be a bad thing if in the attempt to provide ideal physical care there should come a time when the home confinement would not be practicable.

A full explanation of the process of labour and childbirth should be given to the mother by the person to whom she has given her confidence, and this goes a long way towards dispelling such frightening and incorrect information as may have come her way. It is the healthy woman who most needs this and who can make best use of the true facts.

Is it not true that when a healthy and mature woman who is in a healthy relation to her husband and family reaches the moment of childbirth, she is in need of all the immense skill that the nurse has acquired? She is in need of the nurse's presence, and of her power to help in the right way and at the right moment, should something go wrong. But all the same she is in the grip of natural forces and of a process that is as automatic as ingestion, digestion, and elimination, and the more it can be left to nature to get on with it the better it is for the woman and the baby.

One of my patients, who has had two children, and who is now gradually, so it seems, coming through a very difficult treatment in which she herself had to start again – in order to free herself from the influences on her early development of her difficult mother – wrote as follows: '. . . even allowing for the woman to be fairly emotionally mature, the whole process of labour and childbirth breaks down so many controls that one wants all the care, consideration, encouragement and familiarity of the one person looking after you, as a child needs a mother to see it through (each) one of the new and big experiences encountered in its development.'

Nevertheless, with reference to the natural process of childbirth one thing can seldom be forgotten, the fact that the human infant has an absurdly big head.

THE UNHEALTHY MOTHER

In contrast to the healthy, mature woman who comes under the midwife's care there is the woman who is ill, that is, emotionally immature, or not orientated to the part the woman plays in nature's comic opera; or who is perhaps depressed, anxious, suspicious, or just muddled. In such cases, the nurse must be able to make a diagnosis, and here is another reason why she needs to know her patient before she gets into the special and uncomfortable state that belongs to late pregnancy. The midwife certainly needs special training in the diagnosis of psychiatrically ill adults, so that she may be free to treat as healthy those who are healthy. Naturally the immature or otherwise un-healthy mother needs help in some special way from the person who has charge of her case: where the normal woman needs instruction, the ill one needs reassurance; the ill mother may test the nurse's tolerance and make herself a positive nuisance, and perhaps she may need to be restrained if she should become maniacal. But this is rather a matter of common sense, of meeting need with appropriate action, or studied inaction.

In the case of the healthy mother and father, the ordinary case, the midwife is the employee, and she has the satisfaction of being able to give the help that she is employed to give. In the case of the mother who is in some way ill, who is unable to be fully adult, the midwife is the nurse acting with the doctor in the management of a patient – her employer is the agency, the hospital service. It would be terrible if this adaptation to ill health should ever swamp a natural procedure adapted not to illness but to life.

Of course many patients come in between the two extremes I have devised for descriptive purposes. What I wish to emphasize is that the observation that many mothers are hysterical or fussy or self-destructive should not make midwives fail to give health its due and emotional maturity its place; should not lead them to class all their patients as childish, when in fact the majority are fully capable except in the actual matters which they must be able to leave to the nurse. For the best are healthy; it is the healthy women who are the mothers and wives (and midwives) who add richness to mere efficiency, add the positive gain to the routine that is successful merely because it is without mishap.

MANAGEMENT OF THE MOTHER WITH HER BABY

Let us now consider the management of the mother after the birth, in her first relationship to the new-born baby. How is it that when we give mothers a chance to speak freely and to remember back we so often come across a com-ment of the following kind? (I quote from a case description given by a colleague, but time after time I myself have been told the same.)

'He had a normal birth and his parents wanted him. Apparently he sucked well immediately after delivery but was not actually put to the breast for thirty-six hours. He was then difficult and sleepy, and for the next fortnight the feeding situation was most unsatisfactory. Mother felt that the nurses were unsympathetic, that they didn't leave her long enough with the baby. She says that they forced his mouth onto the breast, held his chin to make him suck, and pinched his nose to take him off the breast. When she had him at home she felt that she established normal breast-feeding without any difficulty.'

I do not know whether nurses know that this is how women complain. Perhaps they are never in the position to hear their remarks, and of course mothers are not likely to complain to the nurse to whom they certainly owe much. Also, I must not believe that what mothers say to me gives an accurate picture. I must be prepared to find the imagination at work, as indeed it ought to be, since we are not just bundles of facts; and what our experiences feel like to us and the way they get interwoven with our dreams is all part of the total thing called life, and individual experience.

Sensitive Post-natal State
In our specialized psycho-analytic work we do find that the mother who has just had a baby is in a very sensitive state, and that she is very liable for a week or two to believe in the existence of a woman who is a persecutor. I believe there is a corresponding tendency that we must allow for in the midwife, who can easily at this time slip over into becoming a dominating figure. Certainly it often happens that the two things meet: a mother who feels persecuted and a monthly nurse who drives on as if actuated by fear rather than by love.

This complex state of affairs is often resolved at home by the mother's dismissal of the nurse, a painful procedure for all concerned. Worse than that is the alternative by which the nurse wins, so to speak: the mother sinks back into hopeless compliance, and the relationship between the mother and the baby fails to establish itself.

I cannot find words to express what big forces are at work at this critical point, but I can try to explain something of what is going on. There is a most curious thing happening: the mother who is perhaps physically exhausted, and perhaps incontinent, and who is dependent on the nurse and the doctor for skilled attention in many and various ways, is at the same time the one person who can properly introduce the world to the baby in a way that makes sense to the baby. She knows how to do this, not through any training and not through being clever, but just because she is the natural mother. But her natural instincts cannot evolve if she is scared, or if she does not see her baby when it is born, or if the baby is brought to her only at stated times thought by the authorities to be suitable for feeding purposes. It just does not work that way. The mother's milk does not flow like an excretion; it is a response to a stimulus, and the stimulus is the sight and smell and feel of her baby, and the sound of the baby's cry that indicates need. It is all one thing, the mother's care of her baby and the periodic feeding that develops as if it were a means of communication between the two – a song without words.

Two Opposed Properties

Here then we have on the one hand a highly dependent person, the mother, and at the same time and in the same person, *the expert* in that delicate process, the initiation of breast-feeding, and in the whole bustle and fuss of infant care. It is difficult for some nurses to allow for these two opposed properties of the mother, and the result is that they try to bring about the feeding relationship as they would bring about a defecation in the case of loaded rectum. They are attempting the impossible. Very many feeding inhibitions are started in this way; or even when feeding by bottle is eventually instituted this remains a separate thing happening to the infant, and not properly joined up with the total process that is called infant care. In my work I am constantly trying to alter this sort of fault, which in some cases is actually started off in the first days and weeks by a nurse who did not see that though she is an expert in her job, her job does not include making an infant and a mother's breast become related to one another.

Besides, the midwife has feelings, as I have said, and she may find it difficult to stand and watch an infant wasting time at the breast. She feels like shoving the breast into the baby's mouth, or shoving the baby's mouth into the breast, and the baby responds by withdrawing.

There is another point: this is that, almost universally, the mother feels a little, or a lot, that she has stolen her baby from her own mother. This derives from her playing at mothers and fathers, and from her dreams that belong to the time when she was quite a little girl, and her father was her *beau ideal*. And so she may easily feel, and in some cases she *must* feel, that the nurse is the revengeful mother who has come to take the baby away. The nurse need not do anything about this, but it is very helpful if she avoids actually taking the infant away – depriving the mother of that contact which is natural – and, in fact, only presenting the infant to the mother, wrapped in a shawl, at feedtime. This last is not modern practice, but it was common practice till recently.

The dreams and imaginations and the playing that lie behind these problems remain even when the nurse acts in such a way that the mother has a chance to recover her sense of reality, which she naturally does within a few days or weeks. Very occasionally, then, the nurse must expect to be thought to be a persecuting figure, even when she is not so, and even when she is exceptionally understanding and tolerant. It is part of her job to tolerate this fact. In the end the mother will recover, usually, and will come to see the nurse as she is, as a nurse who tries to understand, but who is human and, therefore, not without a limit to her tolerance.

Another point is that the mother, especially if she be somewhat immature herself, or a bit of a deprived child in her own early history, finds it very hard to give up the nurse's care of her, and to be left alone to care for her infant in the very way that she herself needs to be treated. In this way the loss of the support of a good nurse can bring about very real difficulties in the next phase, when the mother leaves the nurse, or the nurse leaves her.

In these ways psycho-analysis, as I see it, brings to midwifery, and to all work involving human relationships, an increase in the respect that individuals feel for each other and for individual rights. Society needs technicians even in medical and nursing care, but where people and not machines are concerned the technician needs to study the way in which people live and imagine and grow on experience.

14

Advising Parents

The title of this section is perhaps rather misleading. All my professional life I have avoided giving advice, and, if I succeed in my purpose here, the result will be not that other workers will know better how to advise parents, but rather that they will feel less inclined than they may do now to give advice at all.

However, I have no wish to carry this attitude to absurd lengths. If a doctor is asked: 'What shall I do with my child whose illness has been diagnosed as rheumatic fever?' he will advise the parents to put the child to bed and to keep him there until the doctor feels that the danger of heart disease is over. Or if a nurse finds nits in a child's hair she gives instructions which may lead to a satisfactory disinfestation. In other words, in the case of physical illness, doctors and nurses sometimes know the answer because of their special training, and they fail if they do not act accordingly.

But many children who are not physically ill nevertheless come under our care; for instance in maternity cases the work is not curative, because mother and baby are usually healthy. Health is much more difficult to deal with than disease. It is interesting that doctors and nurses may feel bewildered when they are faced with problems that do not relate to physical disease or deformity; they have had no training in healthiness that is comparable to their training in ill health or definite disease.

My observations on the subject of giving advice fall into three categories:

1. The difference between treatment of disease and advice about life.
2. The need to contain the problem in oneself rather than to offer a solution.
3. The professional interview.

TREATMENT OF DISEASE AND ADVICE ABOUT LIFE

As doctors and nurses today become increasingly concerned with psychology, or the emotional or feeling side of life, they need to learn one thing, which is that they are not experts in psychology. In other words, they must adopt quite a different technique with parents as soon as they arrive at the border between the two territories, those of physical disease and of living processes. Let me give a crude example:

114

A paediatrician sees a child because of some condition of the glands in the child's neck. He makes his diagnosis, and informs the mother, giving her the diagnosis and the outline of the proposed treatment. The mother and the child like this paediatrician because he is kind and sympathetic and because he handled the child well during the physical examination. The doctor, being up to date, gives the mother time to talk a little about herself and her home. The mother remarks that the boy is not really happy at school, and tends to get bullied; she is wondering whether to change the boy's school. All is well up to this point, but now the doctor, accustomed to giving advice in his own field, says to the mother: 'Yes, I think it would be good to change the school.'

At this point the doctor has stepped outside his domain, but he has carried with him his authoritarian attitude. The mother does not know it, but he advised a change of school only because he had recently changed the school of one of his own children who had been getting bullied, and so the idea was fresh in his mind. Another kind of personal experience would have made him advise against a change of school. In fact, the doctor was not in a position to give advice. While he was listening to the mother's story he was performing a useful function, without knowing it, and then he behaved in an irresponsible way and advised, and quite unnecessarily too, since he had not been asked.

This sort of thing happens all the time, in medical and nursing practice, and it can be stopped if only doctors and nurses understand that they do not have to settle problems of *living* for their clients, men and women who are often more mature persons than the doctor or nurse who is advising.

The following example illustrates an alternative method:

Two young parents came to see a doctor about their second infant, aged eight months. The baby 'would not wean'. There was no illness. In the course of an hour it emerged that the mother's mother had sent her to the doctor. In fact the grandmother had had difficulty in weaning the infant's mother. There was a depressed mood in the background, both in the grandmother and in the mother. As all this emerged the mother was surprised to find herself crying copious tears.

The resolution of this problem was brought about by the mother's recognition that the problem lay in her relation to her own mother – after this she could get on with the practical problems of the weaning, which necessitated her being able to be unkind to her infant as well as to love her. Advice would not have helped much, because the problem was one of an emotional readjustment.

In contrast, this next incident concerns a girl whom I saw when she was ten years old:

115

The trouble was that she, an only child, had been giving her parents a bad time, though she was very fond of them. A careful history-taking showed that the difficulties started when the child was weaned at eight months. She had done very well, but never became able to enjoy food after leaving the breast. At three she was taken to a doctor, who unfortunately failed to see that the child was in need of personal help. She was already restless, unable to persevere in play, and all the time a nuisance. The doctor said: 'Cheer up, mother, she'll soon be four!'

In another instance, the parents had a consultation with a paediatrician at the time that they were experiencing a weaning difficulty:

This doctor examined and found nothing wrong, and quite rightly told the parents so. But he went further. He told the mother to complete the weaning immediately, which she did.

This advice was neither good nor bad, it was just simply out of place. It cut right across the mother's unconscious conflict about weaning the child, the only one she was likely to have (she was thirty-eight). Of course she took the specialist's advice; what else could she do? – but he ought never to have given it. He should have stuck to his limited job and should have handed over the understanding of the weaning difficulty to someone who could stretch out and around this much wider problem of living and of relationships.

This kind of thing is not, unfortunately, rare; it is a matter of everyday medical practice. I give another example, at rather greater length:

I was rung up by a woman who said that she was involved with a children's hospital, but wanted to talk about her baby in a different way. An appointment was made and she came with her baby, who was nearly seven months old. The young mother sat in the chair with her baby on her lap, and I was very easily able to establish the conditions which I need for observing a baby of this age. I mean that I was able to talk to the mother and yet to deal with the baby without her help or her interference. It quickly became apparent that she was a rather normal sort of person with a feeling for her baby which was easy. There was no jigging up and down of the baby on her knee and nothing false.

The birth of the baby had been straightforward. The baby was 'born sleepy'; it was very difficult to get her to take; in fact she would not wake. The mother described how an attempt was made in the maternity ward to force the infant to take. She wanted to feed her baby by breast and felt that she could do so. She expressed the breast milk, which was given by bottle for a week. The sister was determined to make the child take, and tried incessantly pushing the teat of the bottle in and out of the child's mouth, tickling the child's toes, and jigging the child up and down. All these pro-

116

cedures had no effect and the pattern persisted, so that, even much later on, the mother found that whenever she did anything active in regard to the feeding of the infant this sent the child to sleep. At the end of one week an attempt was made at breast-feeding, but the mother was not allowed to use her intuitive understanding of the infant's needs. It was extremely painful to her. She felt that no one really wanted it to succeed. She had to sit up and take no part while the sister did all she could to make the infant feed. The sister, ordinarily kind and skilled, grasped the child's head and pushed it against the breast and so on. After a little of this, which only produced deeper sleep, breast-feeding was given up and there was a noticeable deterioration following this distorted attempt.

Rather suddenly, at two and a half weeks, there was an improvement. At a month the baby was 6 lb 6 oz (6 lb 9¾ oz at birth) and went home with the mother. The mother was told to feed the baby with a spoon.

The mother had on her own discovered that she could feed her baby perfectly well, although by this time the breast had ceased to function. She was feeding the baby for one and a half hours at a time, and then she switched over to being ready to give multiple small feeds. But by this time a children's hospital had become concerned with the child because of certain physical abnormalities, and advice was given in the hospital outpatient department. This advice seemed to be based on the idea that the mother must be fed up, whereas in fact she was enjoying feeding her baby, and did not mind at all that it was a difficult art. She had to defy the doctors who gave her advice. (Her comment at this point was: 'Definitely the next time I am not having my baby in hospital.') Innumerable investigations were carried out at the hospital in spite of the mother's protests, but naturally she felt that she must leave the physical side to the doctors. There was a shortening of the left forearm, and a cleft palate involving the soft tissues only.

On account of the physical abnormalities the mother felt it necessary to keep under the children's hospital, but this meant that she had to stand being given advice about the feeding of the baby, advice which was usually based on a misunderstanding of her own attitude. She was told to give solids at three months to save herself the trouble of the long feeds or the frequent feeds. This was of no use, and she left over the matter of the introduction of solids. The baby at seven months had begun to want solids, as a result of sitting propped up while the parents ate. She was allowed an occasional titbit and so gradually had the idea that there was another kind of food. Meanwhile she had been fed on milk and chocolate pudding, and weighed 14 lb 4 oz.

Why did the mother come to see me? She found that she wanted support for her own idea of her infant. First, the infant was fully developed for

117

her age, that is to say, not in any way backward, whereas there had been vague suggestions at the hospital that the child might be backward. Second, she was quite willing to accept the deformity of the forearm but not to accept having innumerable investigations, and especially she refused to have the child's arm in a splint. It is evident that the mother felt about her infant's needs in a more sensitive way than the doctors and nurses could hope to feel. For instance, she had been alarmed when the hospital asked to have the baby in for one night simply to have a blood test done. This she disallowed, and the hospital carried out the investigations in the outpatient department without the further complication of having the baby in the ward.

The problem therefore with this mother was that she recognized very clearly her dependence on the hospital on the physical side, and she was engaged in trying to deal with the fact that the physically-minded specialists had not come round to the idea that the baby was yet a human being. At one point when she protested against the splinting of the arm during the early weeks of the child's life she was definitely told that this baby was not yet able to be affected by things happening to it, although she felt quite certain that the baby was in fact adversely affected by the complication of the splint; she could see, in fact, that the infant would be left-handed, and that the splint must hamper the left hand at a vitally important stage, in which reaching out and grasping are creating the world.

Here is a picture of the baby (nearly seven months) at the consultation:

As I came into the room the baby fixed me with her eyes. As soon as she felt I was in communication with her she smiled and clearly felt as if she were communicating with a person. I took an unsharpened pencil and held it in front of her. Still looking at me, and smiling and watching me, she took the pencil with her right hand and without hesitation put it to her mouth where she enjoyed it. In a few moments she used her left hand to help, and then she held it in her left hand instead of in the right hand while mouthing it. Saliva was flowing. All this continued in one way and another until, after five minutes, in the usual way she dropped the pencil by mistake. I returned the pencil and the game re-started. After another few minutes the pencil dropped again, less obviously by mistake. She was now not entirely concerned with putting it in her mouth and at one stage put it between her legs. She was dressed, since I had not thought it necessary to undress her. The third time she dropped the pencil deliberately and watched it go. The fourth time she put it down near her mother's breast and dropped it between the mother and the arm of the chair.

By this time we were near the end of the consultation, which lasted half an hour. When the pencil play had come to an end the baby had had enough and began to whimper, and there were necessarily an awkward few

minutes at the end with the baby feeling that it would be natural to ç   ...
the mother not quite ready to do so. There was no difficulty, and the
mother and baby went out of the room fully contented with each other.

While all this was going on I was talking to the mother and only once did
I have to ask her not to translate what we were talking about in terms of
moving the baby; for instance, when I asked about the wrist she naturally
went to turn up the sleeve.

The consultation achieved no great purpose except in so far as the mother
got support where she needed it. She needed support in regard to her very
real understanding of her own infant, which had to be defended on account
of the inability of the physical doctors to recognize the boundary of their
speciality.

A more general criticism is expressed by a nurse who wrote:

> I have worked for long periods at a famous private maternity home. I have
> seen babies herded together, cots touching, shut up in a stifling airless
> room all night, no attention being paid to their cries. I have seen mothers,
> their babies just brought to them for their feeds, all trussed up with
> nappies round their necks, and their arms pinned down, the baby's mouth
> held to the mother's breast by the nurse, trying to make it feed, sometimes
> for an hour, until the mother is exhausted and in tears. Many mothers had
> never seen their own babies' toes. Mothers with their own 'special' nurses
> fared equally badly. I have seen many cases of definite cruelty to the baby
> by the nurse. In most cases any doctor's orders are ignored.

The fact is that in health we are constantly engaged in keeping time with
natural processes; hurry or delay is interference. Moreover, if we can adjust
ourselves to these natural processes we can leave most of the complex
mechanisms to nature, while we sit back and watch and learn.

THE PROBLEM CONTAINED WITHIN ONESELF

I have already introduced this theme in my illustrations. It can be stated in
this way. Those who have been trained in physical medicine have their own
special skills. The question is, should they or should they not go outside their
special skill and enter the field of psychology, that is to say, of life and living?
My answer is this. Yes, if they can gather into themselves and contain the
personal, family, or social problems that they meet, and so allow a solution
to arrive of its own accord. This will mean suffering. It is a matter of enduring
the worry or even the agony of a case history, of conflict within the individual,
of inhibitions and frustrations, of family discord, of economic hardship,
and it is not necessary to be a psychology student to be useful. One hands back

what one has temporarily held, and then one has done the best that can be done to help. If, on the other hand, it is in a person's temperament to act, to advise, to interfere, to bring about the sort of changes he or she feels would be good, then the answer is: no, this person should not step outside his or her speciality, which concerns physical disease.

I have a friend who does marriage counselling. She has not had much training except as a teacher, but she has a temperament which allows her to accept, during the counselling hour, the problem as it is given her. She does not need to probe to see if the facts are correct and whether the problem is being presented in a one-sided way; she simply takes over whatever comes, and suffers it all. And then the client goes away home somehow feeling different, and often even finding a solution to a problem that had seemed hopeless. Her work is better than that of many who have been given special training. She practically never gives advice, because she does not know what advice to give, and she is not that kind of a person.

In other words, those who find themselves stepping outside the area of their special skill can perform a valuable function if they can immediately stop giving advice.

THE PROFESSIONAL INTERVIEW

Psychology if practised at all must be done within a framework. An interview must be arranged in a proper setting, and a time limit must be set. Within this framework we can be reliable, much more reliable than we are in our daily lives. Being reliable in all respects is the chief quality we need. This means not only that we respect the client's person and his or her right to time and concern. We have our own sense of values, and so we are able to leave the client's sense of right and wrong as we find it. Moral judgement, if expressed, destroys the professional relationship absolutely and irrevocably. The time limit of the professional interview is for our own use; the prospect of the end of the session deals in advance with our own resentment, which would otherwise creep in and spoil the operation of our genuine concern.

Those who practise psychology in this way, accepting limits, and suffering for limited periods of time the agonies of the case, need not know much. But they will learn; they will be taught by their clients. It is my belief that the more they learn in this way the richer they will become, and the less they will feel inclined to give advice.

15

Casewer with Mentally Ill Children

CASEWORK AND PSYCHOTHERAPY

Let me begin by clarifying the usage of the term 'casework' at the present stage of our social service training. Casework is described as *a problem-solving process*. A problem presents itself, and the word casework is used to describe the total function of a particular agency in meeting that problem. Quite another thing is psychotherapy, and often a psychotherapy is carried through with no accompanying casework, since the child patient is brought by adults who recognize illness, and the adult patient can do his or her own casework when freed from the inhibitions, compulsions, mood swings, and so on, which derive their energy from unconscious emotional conflicts.

These two processes, casework and psychotherapy, often coexist in practice and indeed become mutually dependent, but it is important to note both that casework cannot be usefully employed to bolster or patch up a failing therapy, and that it cannot slip over into psychotherapy without getting into a muddle.

Of the two, casework and psychotherapy, it is the former that is related specifically to a social provision; that is to say, it is related to a social attitude that is part of the life of the community and of the present-day general sense of social responsibility. Moreover, the caseworker's work is affected by the agency which gives him or her professional backing.[1] The work done by the caseworker varies according to the social provision which has crystallized out into the agency. This limits the work of the caseworker and at the same time determines much of what is done and strengthens the efficacy of the work.

The caseworker should know as much as possible about the unconscious. But in the caseworker's work there is no attempt to alter the course of events by interpretation of the unconscious. At most, the worker verbalizes for the client various phenomena that are in the foreground but not fully compre-hended: 'You have been very ill'; or, 'You feel that if you had larger premises your children's aggressiveness would not be so liable to get them into trouble'; or, 'You fear your neighbours, and you are wondering whether this is justified or whether the fact is that you are liable to this sort of fear'; and so

[1] See Clare Winnicott, *Child Care and Social Work*, Chapter IV (Welwyn: Codicote Press, 1964).

on. By contrast, the work of the psychotherapist is done mainly by interpretation of the unconscious; by the interpretation of the transference neurosis and of a succession of samples of the patient's personal conflict, each sample being appropriate at the moment in the professional setting of the therapy.

My work has always been divided into four parts. The first belongs to my position as physician in a children's hospital. It is the attempt to meet social need in an outpatient department, and my clinic at the Paddington Green Children's Hospital has become notorious as a psychiatric snack-bar.

The second has been the work that we carry out in the psychology department at Paddington Green, where we take cases from the snack-bar when the psychiatric social workers have room for new patients. Here I suppose we are more definitely doing casework.

Then my third interest has been the psycho-analysis of children, and the training of men and women to do this work.

Lastly, there has been all along my private practice in child psychiatry. Private practice is perhaps the most satisfactory, because there I take full responsibility unless I definitely call in help. My failures, and these are many, are definitely my failures, and they stare me in the face. In my private child-psychiatry practice I suppose I am a caseworker.

In private practice the need for economy is usually evident; and in clinic practice my slogan has always been: how little need be done? Casework can be very economical. Often, however, it is very time-consuming, very worrying, very disappointing.

CLINICAL EXAMPLES

I have tried to select, out of thousands of cases, a graded series of examples to which I shall make brief reference. The first is that of Rupert:

> Rupert, a boy of fifteen, highly intelligent, and seriously depressed, is a bad case of anorexia nervosa. He asked for psycho-analysis, and he is having it. Here there is a minimum of casework, the parents having placed the analyst at the centre of the case. What the analyst needs gains support from the parents, and this covers the relationship between the analyst and the various paediatricians who from time to time become involved in the case. There is a potential danger here: if the boy becomes very ill indeed the parents may lose their confidence in the analyst and then their function of integrating the various elements in the boy's treatment will be lost.[1]

By way of contrast, I refer to one of my failures, the case of Jenny:

> Jenny, a girl of ten, had colitis. She had had a great deal of attention over a number of years. For a year I had the case under my control and I was giving

[1] The treatment carried out by a colleague was successful.

psychotherapy. The treatment was going well, and for this reason the parents had full confidence in me, and I was not aware of the tremendous complications that lay hidden in the background. If I had known that the ill person in this family was the mother and that the girl's illness was quite largely an expression of a severe psychiatric disturbance in the mother, I would have been doing casework along with some psychotherapy, or perhaps instead of it.

As it was, my treatment of the child was interrupted by a renewal of the symptoms associated with the child's return to school. I had no idea at the time that this mother was unable to allow her child to get well enough to go to school, though I knew that she herself had been unable to get to school at exactly this girl's age. I ought to have made a more serious attempt to deal with the mother's problems but I was put off by the fact that the mother was quite unaware of having personal problems, and also by the fact that the girl's symptoms had almost magically disappeared from the start of my psychotherapy of her. The breakdown revealed that the mother when not an integrating force was a violently disintegrating force in this case. I discovered that more and more doctors and other people who felt that they could heal ill children were being employed, even at the same time that the girl was being brought to me. Eventually I fell out of the case.

Here at the centre was a mother who, without knowing it, had it in her to scatter the responsible agents, to make it impossible for any one person to be in control. The child knew that she had no way of dealing with this tendency in her mother, and she gradually adapted herself to fate and got a considerable amount of secondary gain out of being hopelessly ill.

This is a sad state of affairs, and it illustrates something which I constantly come to when thinking about the problem of casework and mentally ill children. I find that the development of the theme brings me again and again to the words *integration* and *disintegration*.

At first it would seem as if there are simply the two processes, psychotherapy and casework. As we look a little closer, we find that along with psychotherapy there is always some casework. There is always something to be done with the parents of the child, or in the provision of alternatives if the home is in some way unsatisfactory. The school perhaps must be kept informed. In some cases the therapist is influenced by the results of discussions with parents, schoolteachers, and various other people who know the child. The word casework seems to be rather loosely applied to all this that is done in the management of a case, which is not psychotherapy.

One begins to wonder what it is that sometimes makes casework vitally important. We can switch over to the other extreme, the case in which the environment has broken down. Here of course the need for management becomes obvious. I think, however, that we do not arrive at the idea of case-work until we recognize that there can be disintegrating forces in the case, and that it is these disintegrating elements which have to be held by some kind of integrating process. In this way the word casework begins to take on a new meaning. The work being done is perhaps the same, but here casework be-comes related to something which is dynamically opposed to it, something which I have tried to illustrate by citing the case of Jenny, whose mother, without being aware, was able to keep her daughter from getting the full benefit of therapy. The disruptive element brings into being and maintains the dynamics of the casework.

This matter of the disintegrating element may be further observed in the examples that follow.

Jeremy, aged eight, was healthy and strong, but he could not get to sleep without holding on to his mother's ear. The family was a good one. The parents had every intention of keeping the home going, and they brought this problem for us to solve.

This was a case in which I handed the whole management to a psychiatric social worker, and in fact I find that this is how I use such workers; I tend to hand over the case to them temporarily, giving them full professional backing, not requiring of them notes on the case, but simply expecting them to report to me from time to time, letting me know that the case is stuck, or that it is finished.

In this instance the social worker was able to deal with the mother's lack of understanding of the part she was playing in the production and mainten-ance of the boy's symptom. Here indeed was a case in which a healthy boy was caught up in his anxiety about his mother's depression. He was an only child, and he found it impossible to free himself from his mother's need of him. At the present time this boy has been able to go away to school, which he enjoys very much, except in so far as he is worrying that his mother is missing him. His mother, however, is dealing with her great loss, and I think she is turning again to her husband in a way that she has not done since the boy was born. In this way the problem is solving itself.

The casework here was in the understanding of this problem by the psychiatric social worker, and in her discussion of the problem with the mother, and also in the interest in the case sustained over a period of time. The parents brought this problem to be solved, and they have confidence in myself and the social worker and the clinic. What I want to emphasize is that this case is held together by the parents. Should we lose their confi-dence, then they would no longer hold together the helping forces which are at present represented by my social worker, with myself in the background.

I think it is possible to divide our cases therefore into three sections:

(i) Those integrated from within.
(ii) Those containing a disintegrating element.
(iii) Those cases that are characterized by an environmental breakdown which has already become a fact.

In the first of these groups the work done implements that which the parents do or would do. In the second the casework needs to develop a dynamic to meet the disintegrating element. In the third the caseworker organizes or reorganizes the environment. Obviously it is the second group that sets us the most severe problem, and often we must fail because we lack authority to do work.

Here is a type of case which can be examined at this point:

A mother brings James, a boy of eight, because he wets himself, and because he won't learn if he does not want to and because he runs away from new situations and from people and from all reality. The mother says that his father is a man of severe moods, and these moods have caused tension in the home. Also, the father has tended to take the boy's side against the mother whenever the mother has had to be firm. In going into the case in great detail, I find a mending situation. The father has gone off and is busy establishing a new family; the mother has a chance to get the boy more clearly into touch with reality; and the boy has begun to use other men in the family as father-substitutes. He obviously likes it when these men are in support of the mother, instead of supporting him against the mother. He is fond of them, and he is generally happier and more at ease than he has been for a long time. Along with all this, his symptoms are starting to lessen in degree.

In this case, therefore, I decided not to see the boy. The mother seemed very relieved when I was able to show her that she was holding a situation in which the boy was able to begin to recover from some of the ill effects of his father's attitude, and it appeared that the boy had in him the health to do this. If I had interfered I would have spoiled the mother's satisfaction, to which she is entitled because of her ability to help her own boy. On the other hand, I am in the background and well able to take part if I am asked to do so, because I have already taken a careful history and I have formed my opinion in regard to the dynamics of the case. If I come in on this case, if I interview the boy, I must either fail or else become a rather important father-substitute. In the latter case I must be able to continue as a substitute until I am no longer wanted, otherwise I am doing harm.

Let us look now at the case of Anthony:

This is a boy who was first seen at the age of eight in my hospital clinic. He is now a man; that is to say, he is somewhere in the world and I am not quite sure where he is. I do not yet know whether there has been a successful outcome to this long case, which has needed all the resources of the clinic. There has been nothing continuous in this boy's life except the existence of my clinic. In the course of his long history the whole staff of the clinic except myself has changed many times. Throughout these many years the department has continued to integrate this boy's environmental provision; nothing else has been positive continuously over the whole period.

The boy's mother took him away from his father when he was a little boy, but she started to live a life of her own and she sent him back to the father when he was about three or four. The father was a very unstable man with a manic-depressive temperament and an exasperating attitude to society. By the time I came in on the case he had married again and had a daughter, and Anthony was brought by his father and stepmother. The stepmother fully supported the father and seemed at the time to be entirely identified with his point of view, with its curious mixture of antagonism to society and a claim that society and not he should educate the boy who obviously had it in him to be brilliant. The boy's IQ is exceptionally high, as we found when we tested it at a later date.

Perhaps the main difficulty in this case has been to avoid letting exasperation with these parents (that is to say, with the father) interfere with a positive attitude towards the boy. The boy was very unprepossessing; apart from having a squint he was miserable-looking and seemed to have nothing nice about him at all. It was a social worker who was giving him psychotherapy who first pointed out to me that the boy was really quite nice when dealt with individually and given a chance to display himself. He had a very strong tendency to steal, and to tell lies, and he was brought to me originally for a compulsion in regard to his faeces and his play with them. It was impossible for his stepmother to keep him in the flat with her daughter; and this was also rendered more impossible by the fact that these two parents would never get a flat that was big enough, although they could afford it, so that there was never any room for the boy, who obviously could not be put into a room to sleep with his half-sister.

The attitude of the parents was one of blaming us or anyone to whom they could speak about the whole situation. They wanted the boy to go to a famous public school and to be prepared for this, and they fully intended to pay nothing for it. The father had never ceased to blame me for sending the boy to a hostel for maladjusted children. Before we got him there, however, we had to find someone to take him who could stand the filthiness of his compulsion. There were very many changes, but always the clinic kept in touch with him and with the people who were looking after him. Throughout this long period the London County Council paid for the boy, who had a really good education. Even the LCC, however, had to be helped in its various departments, administrative and other, by letters from my clinic pointing out that the boy must not be denied the help that could be given simply because the father was very ill and an exasperating person. Eventually the stepmother left the father, and she then became quite a different person and was able to give us a more objective view than we had had before of the father's attitude and of the extremely difficult or impossible position that the boy was constantly in.

This boy was determined to try for a scholarship at one of the two universities which he considered were worthy of him. First he tried Cambridge and failed, and then he tried Oxford, and I think he failed again, but he has never let me know. He did, however, need help at the last minute in order to go in for these scholarships, because his father was incapable of giving support at any moment when it was needed. On this occasion my clinic gave the boy £10, which made it possible for him to take the examination. I think that there is no doubt that he failed and that one day he will come into our lives again when he has established himself in some commercial firm as a research physicist. He could have done well at the university, no doubt, but something hanging over from the father's attitude made him determined to get to either Oxford or Cambridge, and for these universities he was not really suited, because of his history and because of some residual symptoms which no doubt indicate a repressed homosexuality and an unconscious tie-up with the father's personality with all its difficulties.

The amount of work that this case has involved is fairly large; there is a heavy file, and letters to every possible authority go to make up the weight of it. Perhaps the whole case is a failure, and the boy may become no more than a gentleman crook. We cannot tell, but we had to go on providing something integrated and continuous for him, otherwise he was destined for delinquency and a life of crime. Of all the examples so far, this is the one that best illustrates casework. The LCC paid out a very large sum of money in keeping the boy at the sort of school which was good enough if measured against his intellectual capacity. It is not part of casework to provide money, although, as I have said, we did give the boy £10 from a special fund at the very last moment, when his father failed him in a way that seemed impossible from a father, even one so ill as this.

The disintegrating factor in this case was the father's exasperating attitude to society. There was no one that he failed to exasperate. I am not usually ruffled when parents are difficult, but in this case I told the man what I thought of him in such terms that he got in touch with the Minister of Health who, through his officials at the Ministry, got in touch with St. Mary's Hospital, which got in touch with Paddington Green, which eventually got in touch with me. I answered the charge brought against me by saying that I had indeed said what I was accused of saying, and I sent along the file giving the Minister full permission to read it through. So far I have heard no more and the file has been returned.

It might be questioned whether this work we are doing is worth while, but my answer would be that we cannot avoid doing it; if the case comes our way, it is necessary to meet the needs as they appear and to supply what is missing in the environmental provision. We cannot simply work according to our estimate of the result. In many cases our work is interrupted by forces beyond our control, and I suppose that it is a favourable sign that this boy himself has until recently kept us informed about himself, and by this means he has enabled us to continue the casework which we started so long ago. Perhaps it will be just this fact that we have existed in this way over this long period of time that will make the difference between his becoming a criminal or a research worker in physics.

I ought to mention that this boy had some psychotherapy early on in our management of the case. We would have given him psychotherapy of the deepest possible kind if it had been in our power to do so, but there are no placements for children of this kind in the neighbourhood where we work. This example illustrates the overriding need we have at certain times for what I would call a mental hospital for children, one with really good educational facilities, situated not far from our clinic. In this way we could immediately provide psycho-analytic treatment for cases that are having to be managed in hostels for maladjusted children. We could of course only deal with a very small number, but at any rate we could be building up experience. At the present time, if there is a great deal of casework to be done and if a new environment has to be provided, then the child has to leave the area in which psychotherapy is available.

I offer the next example as an illustration of the fact that there is a very close link between the milder forms of psychosis and the early stages of the antisocial tendency. In this case also some stealing occurred.

It concerns a boy at a public school. He was told by his headmaster that he must leave at the age of sixteen because he was stealing in a big way. This was a very sad matter because the boy was at a school where his own father had been and there were special reasons therefore why the school should want to do well for this boy. The father was a housemaster at another school. In an interview with the boy, I found that he was able to describe to me a very difficult time that he went through when he was about five or six years old, when his parents seemed to him to be neglecting him. I spoke to the parents about this and they said that it was perfectly true that at this age the boy was not treated as he should have been. It had taken the parents some time to see that they had been neglecting him, and when they had seen it they had done everything they could to make up for it. This was just at the time when the boy, who had been the younger brother and rather made a fuss of, became a middle child because of the birth of a sister.

The home in this case is a very good one, and the parents were greatly distressed to find that what they had done had laid the basis for the boy's breakdown at public school. They were only too willing to take him home and to let him have the whole of them, while the other two children were away at their respective schools. The parents acted as they said they would, and gave the boy a really good year with no responsibilities. At the end of this year he began to want to go to school, but not before he had made a rather severe regression and had become extremely dependent like a small child, but not in this case like an infant. He eventually went to day-school, and then he gradually decided to go to the school at which his father is a housemaster, although becoming a boarder in another house. Soon the fact that he had been stealing was forgotten, and indeed he has never stolen since the day that I had the hour with him, in which he remembered his very severe depression belonging to this period of neglect when he was five years of age.

Here was an illness that was not psychoneurosis and the treatment was not psychotherapy. It was a kind of casework, I suppose, the way I dealt with the parents, let them know of their power to help, and kept in touch with their varying needs as the boy first got more ill (but not with a return of stealing) and then recovered. In this instance the casework was made simple by the fact that the parents and the headmaster of the school were only wanting the boy's recovery, so that there was no disintegrating factor to be met and countered. There was no disruptive element making the casework into a reactive holding process.

In some cases of childhood psychosis, especially the severe cases, there is an abnormal parental attitude which is in fact the cause of the illness and which continues as a factor maintaining the illness. In this way the illnesses of child and parent interact, and great distress ensues. In such situations casework aims at relief through the finding of alternative accommodation. But, how difficult!

CASEWORK AND TEAMWORK

I conclude this section with some observations that have to do with a more administrative aspect of the problem of casework with mentally ill children –

that is, the relationship between casework and the team as it is employed in the child guidance clinic (i.e. psychiatrist, psychologist, and psychiatric social worker).

Some people feel, I think, that casework is being done when the routine of child guidance comes into play. But the term casework does not justify itself if it simply applies to the complexity that arises from teamwork. My own point of view is this, that the child-guidance team and the routine of the child-guidance clinic are well adapted to the investigation of a case in which a report is needed for a juvenile court. This work, however, has nothing to do with casework, which may or may not be done alongside investigating and reporting.

A lot of the work of the child-guidance clinic consists in reintegrating the several aspects of the case which have been separated out from each other by the existence of the team. Perhaps it is for this reason that I have never personally used the team as it is used in child guidance. In a really good child-guidance clinic the psychiatrist is able at the case conference to reintegrate the various elements of the case, and watching this process is of course very useful for students. Nevertheless, it is possible for a case to be taken to pieces and put together again by a child-guidance clinic and yet for no casework to have been done.

By the way that I happen to have worked I have been able to reap the advantage in recent years of having psychiatric social workers and a psychologist as colleagues, so that we have seen cases together and we have been able to benefit on the principle that two heads are better than one. In a certain number of cases, according to the capacity of the psychiatric social worker to take more work, I have been very glad to hand over, lock, stock, and barrel, either temporarily or on a long-term basis, to such a worker. This is the same as handing over a case to one of my psychiatric colleagues, except that I retain medical responsibility for the case and therefore expect to be kept informed by the social worker of what is happening.

There is one more observation which I think can be useful. Whereas in psychotherapy it is very difficult to change the psychotherapist, in casework it can be, and it should be, the clinic rather than the individual that provides the continuity in the relationship to the case. The caseworker cannot be sure of remaining for ever in one post. There is some loss, if one thinks of the psychotherapy of individuals, through the fact that the caseworker is working for an agency or a clinic. The gain, however, is tremendous, because the clinic has a stability that far exceeds that of any individual. I have given one case to illustrate this point. Of course I do not mean that the relationships between the individuals concerned can ever be toned down in such a way that there is no trauma when there is a change of caseworker. One can imagine an extreme in which the caseworker is no longer a person, and the agency is permanent and no more than an administrative machine. This would take us right back to the dark ages from which we have emerged. In a sense casework is the human and fallible element that uses the administrative machinery but prevents the machinery from using the client. How easy, if one looks at it this way, to see that caseworkers and administrators may suspect each other although the case requires the cooperation of the two.

SUMMARY

I have attempted to rescue the idea of casework from the complex machinery of teamwork.

Casework is not the main feature in the vast majority of cases in which a child is mentally ill. Usually there are parents who recognize the illness in their child and seek treatment for the child. Casework obviously becomes the main feature when a child is mentally ill and at the same time there is an environmental deficiency which has to be made good. I have drawn particular attention to the type of case in which casework takes on a special meaning because of some element in the case which is disruptive.

In the simplest case there is a psychiatric illness in one parent or both, and casework derives its dynamic force and its own integration as a reaction to this illness in the parents. This theme can be developed to cover a wide variety of cases, but the main point is that in some way or other, because of a disintegrating tendency in the case, an actively integrating process must develop if the need of the case is to be met. Here it is not the work done which is important so much as the organization of an actively integrating tendency or a holding[1] of the potentially disruptive case material. I am suggesting that it is here that we best employ the word casework.

This is not a new idea but it needs emphasis, and a sorting out of these various tasks helps us to see more clearly the difference between casework and psychotherapy with the mentally ill child.

[1] For the concept of 'holding' in casework, see Clare Winnicott, *Child Care and Social Work* (Welwyn: Codicote Press, 1964).

16

The Deprived Child and how he can be Compensated for Loss of Family Life

By way of introduction to the subject of providing for the child who has been deprived of family life, let us remember this: that the chief concern of a community should be for its healthy members. It is the usual run of good homes that need priority, for the simple reason that the children who are being nurtured in their own homes are the ones that reward; it is the care of these children that pays the dividends.

Two things follow, if this be accepted. First, provision for the ordinary home of a basic ration of housing, food, clothing, education, and recreation facilities, and what could be called cultural food, has first claim on our attention. Second, we must see that we never interfere with a home that is a going concern, not even for its own good. Doctors are especially liable to get in the way between mothers and infants, or parents and children, always with the best intentions, for the prevention of disease and the promotion of health; and doctors are by no means the only offenders in this respect. For example:

> A mother who had been divorced asked me for advice in the following situation. She had a six-year-old daughter, and a religious organization with which the father of this child was connected wished to take the child away from the mother and put her in a boarding school – for holidays as well as term-time – because this organization did not approve of divorce. The fact that the child was quite settled and secure with the mother and her new husband was to be ignored, and a state of deprivation was to be created for this child because of a principle: a child must not live with a divorced mother.

A great number of deprived children are in fact engineered in one way or another, and the remedy lies in avoidance of bad management.

Nevertheless, I have to face up to the fact that I am myself a deliberate home-breaker, like many others. We are all the time sending children away from their homes. In my clinic alone we have cases every week in which it is urgently necessary to get the child away from home. It is true that such children are seldom under the age of four. Everyone working in this field knows

132

the type of case in which, for one reason or another, a state of affairs has arisen of such a nature that, unless the child is removed within a few days or weeks, the home will break up or the child will certainly get to the courts. Often one can predict that the child will do well away from home or that the home will do well with the child away. There are many distressing cases that mend themselves if one can immediately bring about these separations, and it would be a great pity if all that we are doing to avoid the unnecessary destruction of good homes should in any way weaken the efforts of the authorities that are responsible for the provision of short-term and long-term accommodation for the kind of children that I am considering here.

When I say that in my clinic we have these cases each week, I am implying that in the great majority of cases we manage to help the child in the setting which already exists. This is of course our aim, not only because it is economical but also because when the home is good enough the home is the proper place for the child to grow up in. The vast majority of the children who need psychological help are suffering from disturbances in respect of *internal* factors, disturbances in the emotional development of the individual, disturbances which are largely inherent because life is difficult. These disturbances can be treated with the child at home.

ASSESSMENT OF DEPRIVATION

In order to discover how we can best help a deprived child we first have to determine what amount of normal emotional development was made possible in the beginning by a good-enough environment ((i) infant-mother relationship, (ii) triangular father-mother-child relationship); and then in the light of this to try to assess the damage done by the deprivation, when it began and as it subsequently persisted. The history of the case is therefore important.

The following six categories may be found useful as a way of classifying cases of broken home:

(*a*) Ordinary good home, broken by an accident to one or both parents.

(*b*) Home broken by the separation of the parents, who are good as parents.

(*c*) Home broken by the separation of the parents, who are not good as parents.

(*d*) Home incomplete, because there is no father (child illegitimate). The mother is good; grandparents may take over parental role, or help to some extent.

(*e*) Home incomplete, because there is no father (child illegitimate). The mother is not good.

(*f*) There never was a home.

In addition, cross-classifications will be made:

(*a*) according to the age of the child; and the age at which a good-enough environment ceased;

(*b*) according to the child's nature and intelligence;

(*c*) according to the child's psychiatric diagnosis.

We avoid making any assessment of the problem on the basis of the child's symptoms, or the nuisance value of the child, or the feelings roused in us by the child's plight. These considerations lead us astray. Often the history is lacking or deficient in essential parts. Then, and in fact commonly, the only way to determine the fact of an early good-enough environment is to supply a good environment and see what use the child can make of it.

Here special comment is needed on the meaning of the words 'what use the child can make of a good environment'. A deprived child is ill, and it is never so simple a matter that environmental readjustment will bring about a change-over in the child from ill to healthy. At best, the child who can benefit from a simple environmental provision begins to get better, and as the change takes place from ill to less ill the child becomes increasingly able to be angry about the past deprivation. Hate of the world is there somewhere, and health has not arrived unless the hate has been felt. In a small proportion of cases the hate is felt, and even this small complication can cause difficulties. However, this favourable result comes about only if everything is relatively available to the child's *conscious* self, and this is but seldom the case. To some extent, or to a very great extent, the feelings belonging to the environmental failure are not available to consciousness. Where deprivation occurs on top of a satisfactory early experience something like this *can* happen and the hate appropriate to the deprivation can be reached. The following example illustrates this kind of situation:

Here is a girl of seven. Her father died when she was three but she nego-tiated this difficulty all right. The mother cared for her excellently and married again. This remarriage was successful and the child's stepfather was very fond of her. All was well until the mother became pregnant. At this point the father completely changed in his attitude to the stepdaughter. He became orientated towards his own baby and withdrew affection from the stepchild. After the birth of the baby things got worse, and the mother was in a position of divided loyalties. The child could not thrive in this atmosphere but, removed to a boarding school, she may quite possibly be able to do well and even to understand the difficulty that occurred in her own home.

On the other hand, the next case shows the effects of an unsatisfactory early experience:

A mother brings her little boy of two and a half. He has a good home but he is only happy when having the personal attention of his mother or father. He cannot leave his mother and therefore cannot play on his own, and the approach of strangers is felt by him to be terrifying. What has gone wrong in this case, considering that the parents are ordinary normal people? The fact is that the boy was adopted at five weeks, and already by that time he was ill. There is some evidence that the matron of the home in which he was born made a special pet of him, since she seems to have tried to hide him from these parents who were looking for an infant to adopt. The transfer at five weeks caused a severe upset in the emotional development of the infant, and the adopting parents are only beginning to be able gradually to overcome the difficulties – which they certainly did not expect, taking over a baby at so early a date. (They had in fact tried very hard to get a baby even earlier, in the first week or two of the infant's existence, because they were aware of the complications that could arise.)

We have to know what sort of things happen in the child when a good setting is broken up and also when a good setting has never existed, and this involves a study of the whole subject of the emotional development of the individual. Some of the phenomena are well-enough known: hate is repressed or the capacity to love people is lost. Other defensive organizations become set up in the child's personality. There may be regression to some early phases of the emotional development which were more satisfactory than others, or there may be a state of pathological introversion. Much more commonly than is generally thought, there is a splitting of the personality. In the simplest form of this splitting, the child presents a shop-window or out-turned half, built up on a basis of compliance, and the main part of the self containing all the spontaneity is kept secret and is all the time involved in hidden relationships to idealized fantasy objects.

Although it is difficult to make a simple and clear statement of these phenomena, an understanding of them is necesssay if we are to see what are the favourable signs in the case of deprived children. If we do not understand what is there when the child is very ill, we cannot see, for instance, that a depressed mood in a deprived child may be a favourable sign, especially when not accompanied by strong persecution ideas. A simple depressed mood indicates at any rate that the child has retained unity of personality and has a sense of concern, and is indeed taking responsibility for all that has gone wrong. Also, antisocial acts, such as bed-wetting and stealing, indicate that at any rate momentarily there can be hope – hope of rediscovering a good-enough mother, a good-enough home, a good-enough inter-parental relationship. Even anger may indicate that there is hope, and that for the moment the child is a unit and able to feel the clash between what is conceivable and what is actually to be found in what we call shared reality.

Let us consider the meaning of the antisocial act, for instance, stealing. When a child steals, what is sought (by the total child, i.e. the unconscious included) is not the object stolen; what is sought is the person, the mother, from whom the child has the right to steal because she is the mother. In fact every infant at the start can truly claim the right to steal from the mother because the infant invented the mother, thought her up, created her out of an innate capacity to love. By being there the mother gave her infant, gradually, bit by bit, the person of herself as material for the infant to create into, so that in the end his subjective self-created mother was quite a lot like the mother we can agree about. In the same way, the child who wets the bed is looking for the mother's lap that is meet to be wetted in the early stages of the infant's existence.

The antisocial symptoms are gropings for environmental recovery, and indicate hope. They fail not because they are wrongly directed, but because the child is unconscious of what is going on. The antisocial child needs therefore a specialized environment that has a therapeutic aim, and that can give a reality response to the hope that is expressed in the symptoms. This has to be spread over a long period, however, to become effectual as a therapeutic, since, as I have said, much is unavailable to the child as conscious feeling and memory; and also the child has to gain great confidence in the new environment, in its stability and its capacity for objectivity, before the defences can be given up – defences against intolerable anxiety that is always liable to be reactivated by new deprivation.

We know, then, that the deprived child is an ill person, a person with a past history of traumatic experience, and a personal way of coping with the anxieties roused; and a person with a capacity for recovery greater or less according to the degree of loss of consciousness of the appropriate hate and of the primary capacity to love. What practical measures can be undertaken to help such a child?

PROVIDING FOR THE DEPRIVED CHILD

Obviously someone has to care for the child. The community no longer denies responsibility for children who are deprived; indeed, the swing is right in the other direction today. Public opinion demands that the best that is possible shall be done for the child whose own family life is lacking. Many of our troubles at the present time come from the practical difficulties that arise in the application of the principles deriving from the new attitude.

It is not possible to do the right thing for a child by passing a law or by setting up administrative machinery. These things are necessary but are only the first miserable stage. In every case a proper management of a child involves *human beings*, and these human beings have to be of the right kind; and there is a distinct limit to the number of such people who are immediately available. This number is much increased if in the administrative machinery there is a provision for *intermediate* persons, who can on the one hand deal with the overriding authorities and on the other hand keep in touch with the persons actually doing the work, appreciating their good points, acknowledging success where it occurs, enabling the educative process to leaven and make interesting the job, discussing failures and the reasons for failure, and being available to give relief where necessary by removal of a child from a foster home or hostel, perhaps at short notice. The care of a child is very much a whole-time process, and leaves the person who is doing the work with little emotional reserve for coping with administrative procedure or with the wide social issues represented in certain cases by the police. Conversely, the person who is able to keep one eye firmly on administration or on the police is unlikely to be first-rate in the care of a child.

Coming now to more specific matters, it is necessary to keep in mind the psychiatric diagnosis of every child for whom provision has to be made. As I have pointed out, this diagnosis can be made only after a carefully taken history or perhaps after a period of observation. The point is that a child deprived of family life can have had a good start in infancy and can even have had the beginnings of a family life. The foundation of the mental health of the child may in such a case have been well laid down, so that the illness secondary to the deprivation supervenes on health. On the other hand, another child, not perhaps looking worse, has no healthy experience which can be re-discovered and reactivated by the child in a new environment; and, further than that, there may have been such a poor or complex management of early infancy that the foundations for mental health in terms of personality structure and reality sense may be deficient. In such extreme cases the good environment has to be created for the first time, or a good environment may have no chance at all because the child is fundamentally unsound, perhaps with the addition of a hereditary tendency to insanity or instability. In the extreme cases the child is insane, although this word is not used in respect of children.

It is important to recognize this part of the problem, otherwise those who are assessing results will be surprised to find that with the very best management there are always failures, and always children who grow up eventually to become insane or at best antisocial.

The diagnosis of the child having been made, in terms of the presence or absence of positive features in the early environment and the child's relation to it, the next thing to consider is procedure. I want to emphasize here (and I write as a psycho-analyst of children) that the clear principle of the manage-

137

ment of the deprived child is not the provision of psychotherapy. Psychotherapy is something which eventually, one hopes, may be added in some instances to whatever else is done. At the present time, generally speaking, personal psychotherapy is not practical politics. The essential procedure is the provision of an alternative to the family. We can classify what we provide in the following way:

(i) Foster parents, who wish to give the child a family life like that which the child could have been provided with by the actual parents. It is generally acknowledged that this is the ideal, but one must quickly add that it is essential that children sent to foster parents must be children who can respond to something so good. This practically means that they must have had something of a good-enough family life somewhere in their past and have been able to respond to it. In this foster home they have a chance to rediscover something they have had and have lost.

(ii) Next come the small homes in the care, if possible (but not necessarily), of married wardens, each home containing children in various age groups. Such small homes can conveniently be grouped together, with advantages both from the administrative point of view and from the point of view of the children, who acquire cousins, so to speak, as well as siblings. Here again, the best is being attempted, and therefore it is essential that children who cannot benefit from something so good shall be kept away. One unsuitable child can spoil the good work of a whole group. It must be remembered that good work is emotionally more difficult than less good work, and only too easily, if there is a failure, those in charge give up the best and slip over into the easier and less valuable types of management.

(iii) In the third category the groups are larger. The hostel perhaps contains eighteen. The wardens can keep in personal touch with all the children but they have assistants, and the management of the assistants is an important part of their job. Loyalties are divided and the children have opportunity for putting the grown-ups against each other and playing on latent jealousies. We are already in the direction of the less good management. On the other hand, we are also in the direction of the type of management that can deal with the less satisfactory type of deprived child. The way in which things are worked is less personal, more dictatorial, and the demands made on each child are less. A child in such a home is less in need of a previous good experience which can be revived. In such homes there is less need than there is in the small homes for the child to grow towards the ability to identify with the home while retaining personal impulsiveness and spontaneity. The intermediate thing is good enough in the larger homes, that is to say, a merging of identity with the other children in the group. This involves both loss of personal identity and loss of identification with the total home setting.

(iv) Next in our classification comes the larger hostel, in which the wardens are mainly engaged in the management of the staff and only indirectly concerned with the minute-to-minute management of the children. Here there are advantages in that a larger number of children can be accommodated. The fact that there is a larger staff means that there is more opportunity for discussion among the staff; there are also advantages for the children in that there can be teams competing with each other. I think it can be claimed that this hostel is further in the direction of the type of management that can cope with the more ill children, i.e. those whose good experiences at the beginning were small. The rather impersonal chief can be in the background as a representative of authority which such children need; which they need because within themselves they are incapable of holding both the spontaneity and the control at the same time. (Either they must be identified with authority and turn into miniature gauleiters, or else they must be impulsive, relying entirely on external authority for control.)

(v) Beyond this is the still larger institution which does its best for children under impossible conditions. For some time there will have to be such institutions. They have to be run by dictatorship methods, and what is good for the individual child has to be subordinated on account of the limitations of that which society can provide immediately. Here is a good form of sublimation for potential dictators. One can even find other advantages in this undesirable state of affairs, for, the accent being on dictatorship methods, quite hopelessly difficult children can be managed in such a way that they do not get into trouble with society over long periods. Really ill children can be happier here than in better homes, and they can become able to play and learn, so much so that the uninformed observer must be impressed. It is difficult in such institutions to recognize the children who become ripe to be removed to a more personal type of management, where their growing capacity to identify with society without losing their own individuality can be catered for.

Therapeutics and Management

I now want to contrast the two extremes of management, the one being the foster home and the other the large institution. In the former, as I have said, the aim is truly therapeutic. It is hoped that the child will recover in the course of time from the deprivation which, without such management, would not only leave a scar but would actually leave crippling. If this is to happen, much more is needed than the child's response to the new environment.

At first the child is apt to make a quick response and those concerned are apt to think that their troubles are over. When the child gains confidence, however, there follows a growing capacity for anger with the previous environmental failure. It is unlikely, of course, that what happens will exactly look like this, especially since the child is not conscious of the main revolutionary changes which are taking place. The foster parents will find that they themselves periodically become the target of the child's hate. They will have to take over the anger which is beginning to be able to be felt and which belongs to the failure in the child's own home. It is very important for foster parents to understand this, otherwise they get disheartened; and child care officers must know about it, otherwise they will blame foster parents and believe the children's stories about ill treatment and starvation. If the foster parents receive a visit from an officer who is looking for signs of trouble, they may become over-anxious, and this makes them try to seduce the child into being friendly and happy, thus depriving the child of a most important part of recovery.

Sometimes a child will very cleverly bring about specific ill treatment, in an attempt to bring into the actual present a badness that can be met by hate; the cruel foster parent is then actually loved because of the relief that the child feels through transformation of 'hate versus hate' locked up within into hate meeting external hate now. Unfortunately at this point the foster parents are liable to become misunderstood in their social group.

There are ways out. For instance, some foster parents will be found to work on the rescue principle. For them the child's parents were hopelessly bad, and they say so over and over again out loud to the child, and thus they divert the child's hate from themselves. This method may work fairly well but it ignores the reality situation, and in any case disturbs something which is a feature in deprived children, that they tend to idealize their own home such as it is. No doubt it is more healthy when the foster parents can take the periodical waves of negative feeling and survive them, reaching each time to a new, more secure (because less idealized) relation to the child.

In contrast, the child in the big institution is *not* being managed with the aim of curing him of his illness. The aims are, first, to provide housing and food and clothing for children who are neglected; second, to devise a type of management in which the children live in a state of order rather than chaos; and third, to keep as many of the children as possible from a clash with society until they must be let loose on the world somewhere about the age of sixteen. It is no good mixing things up and pretending that at this end of the scale an attempt is being made to create normal human beings. A strict management in such cases is essential, and if to this can be added some humanity so much the better.

It must be remembered that even in very strict communities, as long as there is consistency and fairness the children can discover humanity among themselves, and they can even come to value the strictness because of the fact that it implies stability. Understanding men and women working this kind of system can find ways of introducing more humane moments. Something can be done, for instance, by selecting suitable children for regular contacts with reliable aunt and uncle substitutes in the outside world. People can be found who will write on the child's birthday, and who will ask the child home to tea three or four times a year. These are only examples but they show the sort of thing that can be done and that is done without disturbance of the strict setting in which the children live. It has to be remembered that if the strict setting is the basis, then it is disturbing to the children if this strict setting has exceptions and loopholes. If there has to be a strict setting, then let it be consistent, reliable, and fair, so that it can have positive value. Besides, there will always be those children who abuse privileges, and then the children who could use them will have to suffer.

In this type of large institution, for the sake of peace and quiet, the accent is put on management on behalf of society. Within this framework the children must lose their own individuality to a greater or lesser extent. (I am not ignoring the fact that in the intermediate institutions there is room for a gradual growth of the children who are healthy enough to grow, so that they become increasingly able to identify with society without loss of identity.)

There will still be some children who, because they are what I want to call mad (although one must not use such a word), are failures even if dictated to. For such children there must be the equivalent of the mental hospital which caters for adults, and I think we have not yet determined what is the best that society can do for these extreme cases. Such children are so ill that those who are looking after them easily recognize that when they begin to become anti-social this means that they are beginning to get better.

I conclude this section by referring two matters which are of great importance in a consideration of the needs of the deprived child.

Importance of Child's Early History
The first of these very much concerns the child care worker, especially in her capacity of boarding out and of keeping a watchful eye on the new situation. If I were a child care officer, as soon as a child came into my care I would immediately want to collect together every particle of information that could be found about that child's life up to the present moment. This is always urgent because the passage of every day makes it less easy for anyone to come by the essential facts. How distressing it was in the second world war, when the failures of the evacuation scheme were being dealt with, and there were children about whom one could never find out anything!

We know how normal children sometimes say as they are going to bed, 'What did I do today?', and then the mother says, 'You woke up at half past six, and you played with your teddy, singing nursery rhymes until we woke,

141

and then you got up and went out into the garden, and then you had break-fast, and then . . .', and so on, until the whole scheme of the day has been integrated from outside. The child has all the information there but likes to be helped to be aware of it all. This feels good and real and helps the child to distinguish reality from the dream and from imaginative play. The same thing writ large would be represented by the way the ordinary parent has of going over the past life of the child, including what the child only just remem-bers and also what the child does not know anything about.

The lack of this simple thing is a serious loss for the deprived child. At any rate there should be someone who has gathered together whatever is available. In the very favourable case the child care officer will be able to have a long interview with the actual mother, letting her gradually unfold the whole his-tory from the moment of birth, even perhaps giving important details about her experiences during pregnancy and the experiences leading up to con-ception, which may or may not have determined much of her attitude to the child. Often, however, the worker will have to go here and there and every-where to collect information; even the name of a friend that the child had in the institution before last may be valuable. There will follow the task of organizing a contact with the child, when the social worker gains the child's confidence. Some way may be found of letting the child know that here or in a file in the office of the children's officer there is the saga of the child's life as lived hitherto. The child may not want to be told anything for the time being, but later on details may be needed. It is particularly the illegitimate and the child with a broken home who eventually need to be able to get to the facts – that is, if health is to be reached, and I assume that in the case of the fostered child the aim is to produce a healthy child. The child at the other extreme, managed by dictatorial methods in a large group, is less likely to become well enough to assimilate the truth about the past.

Because this is so, and because there is an acute shortage of workers, the start should be made at the more normal end. Even so, child care workers are likely to feel that, much as they would like to do this kind of thing, it is impossible because of their case load. My point is that child care workers must decide absolutely that they will not take more cases than they can manage. There is no half and half business about the care of children. It is a matter of dealing with a few children well and handing the others over to the large institution with dictatorial methods until society can manage something better. Good work has to be personal, or it is cruel and tantalizing both to the child and to the child care worker. *The work is only worth doing if it is personal and if those who are doing the work are not overburdened.*

It must be remembered that if child care workers accept too much work they will be bound to have failures, and eventually statisticians will come along and prove that the whole thing is wrong, and that the dictatorial methods are more effectual in providing factories with workers, and homes with domestic servants.

Transitional Phenomena

The other point that I wish to make can be got at again by first looking at the normal child. How is it that ordinary children can be deprived of their homes and of all that is familiar to them without becoming ill? Every day children go into hospital and come out again, not only physically mended but also undisturbed and even enriched by the new experience. Over and over again children go away to stay with aunts and uncles, and in any case they go away with their parents from familiar surrounding to strange ones.

This is a very complex subject, which we may approach in the following way. Let us think of any child whom we know well, and ask ourselves what it is that the child takes to bed to help in the transition from waking to dream life: a doll; several dolls perhaps; a teddy; a book; a bit of mother's old dress; a corner of an eiderdown; a bit of old blanket; or it may be a handkerchief which was substituted for a napkin at a certain stage in the infant's development. In some cases it may be that there was no such object, but the child simply sucked what was available, a fist, and then the thumb or two fingers; or perhaps there was a genital activity to which the word masturbation is more easily applied; or the child may lie on the tummy or make rhythmic movements, showing the orgiastic nature of the experience by sweating in the head. In some cases from early months the infant will have demanded nothing less than the personal appearance of a human being, probably the mother. There is a wide range of possibilities which can be commonly observed. Among the various dolls and teddies belonging to a child, there may be one particular, probably soft, object that was introduced to the infant at about ten, eleven, or twelve months, which the infant treats in a most brutal as well as a most loving manner, and without which the infant could not conceive of going to bed; this thing would certainly not have to be left behind if the child had to go away; and if it were lost it would be a disaster for the child and therefore for those caring for him or her. It is unlikely that such an object would ever be given away to another child, and in any case no other child would want it; eventually it becomes smelly and filthy and yet one dare not wash it.

I call this thing a transitional object. By this means I can illustrate that one difficulty every child experiences is to relate subjective reality to shared reality which can be objectively perceived. From waking to sleeping the child jumps from a perceived world to a self-created world. In between there is a need for all kinds of transitional phenomena – neutral territory. I would describe this precious object by saying that there is a tacit understanding that no one will claim that this real thing is a part of the world, or that it is created by the infant. It is understood that both these things are true: the infant created it and the world supplied it. This is the continuation forward of the initial task which the ordinary mother enables her infant to undertake, when by a most delicate active adaptation she offers herself, perhaps her breast, a thousand times at the moment that the baby is ready to create something like the breast that she offers.

Most of the children who come into the category of the maladjusted either have not had an object of this kind, or they have lost it. There must be someone for the object to stand for, which means that the condition of these children cannot be cured simply by giving them a new object. A child may, however, grow to such confidence in the person who is caring for him or her that objects that are deeply symbolical of that person will appear. This will be felt as a good sign, like being able to remember a dream, or to dream of a real event.

All these transitional objects and transitional phenomena enable the child to stand frustrations and deprivations and the presentation of new situations. Do we make sure in our management of deprived children that we respect such transitional phenomena as do exist! I think that if we look at the use of toys, of auto-erotic activities, of bedtime stories and nursery rhymes in this way, we can see that, by means of these things, children have got a capacity for being deprived to some extent of what they are used to and even of what they need. A child removed from one home to another or from one institution to another may manage or may not manage according to whether a bit of cloth or a soft object can go with him or her from one place to the other; or whether there are familiar rhymes to be said at bedtime that link the past with the present; or whether the auto-erotic activities can be respected and tolerated and even valued because of their positive contribution. Surely with children whose environments are disturbed these phenomena have a special importance, and the study of them should enable us to increase our capacity to give help to these human beings who are being bandied about before they have been able to accept that which we accept only with the greatest difficulty: that the world is never as we would create it and that the best that can happen for any one of us is that there shall have been sufficient overlap of external reality and what we can create. We accept the idea of an identity between the two as an illusion.

It may be hard for people who have had fortunate environmental experiences to understand these things; nevertheless, the infant or the little child who is being moved about from one place to another is coping with exactly this problem. If we deprive a child of the transitional objects and disturb the established transitional phenomena, then the child has only one way out, which is a split in the personality, with one half related to a subjective world and the other reacting on a compliance basis to the world which impinges.

When this split is formed and the bridges between the subjective and the objective are destroyed, or have never been well formed, the child is unable to operate as a total human being.[1]

To some extent this state of affairs can always be found in the child who comes under our care because of being deprived of family life. In the children that we hope to send to foster parents or to the small sensitive hostel there will certainly be found in every case some degree of this splitting. The subjective world has the disadvantage for the child that although it can be ideal it can also be cruel and persecutory. At first the child will translate whatever is found in these terms, and either the foster home is wonderful and the real home is bad, or vice versa. In the end, however, if all goes well, the child will be able to have a fantasy of good and bad homes and to dream and talk about them and to draw them, and at the same time to perceive the real home provided by the foster parents as it is actually.

The actual foster home has the advantage of not swinging violently from good to bad and from bad to good. It remains more or less just middlingly disappointing and middlingly reassuring. Those who are managing deprived children can be helped by recognizing that each child does to some extent bring a capacity for accepting a neutral territory, localized in some way or other into masturbation or the use of a doll or the enjoyment of a nursery rhyme or something like that. So, from the study of what normal children enjoy, we can learn what these deprived children absolutely need.

[1] For a fuller development of this theme, see 'Transitional Objects and Transitional Phenomena', Chapter XVIII in *Collected Papers* by D. W. Winnicott (London: Tavistock Publications, 1958).

17

Group Influences and the Maladjusted Child

The School Aspect

My purpose in this section is to study certain aspects of the psychology of groups, which may help towards a better understanding of the kind of problems that are involved in the group management of maladjusted children. Let us think first of the normal child, who lives in a normal home, has aims, and goes to school actually wanting school to teach; who finds his or her own environment, and even helps to maintain or develop or modify it. In contrast, the maladjusted child needs an environment that has the accent on management rather than on teaching; the teaching is a secondary matter and may at times be a specialized affair, more of the nature of remedial teaching than of instruction in school subjects. In other words, in the case of the maladjusted child, 'school' has the meaning of 'hostel'. For these reasons, those who are concerned with the management of antisocial children are not schoolteachers who add a dash of human understanding here and there; they are in fact group psychotherapists who add a dash of teaching. And so a knowledge of the formation of groups is highly important for their work.

Groups and the psychology of groups constitute a vast subject, out of which I have selected one main thesis for presentation here: namely, that the basis of group psychology is the psychology of the individual, and especially of the individual's personal integration. I start therefore with a brief statement of the task of individual integration.

INDIVIDUAL EMOTIONAL DEVELOPMENT

Psychology emerged from a hopeless muddle with the now accepted idea that there is a continuous process of emotional development, starting before birth, and continuing throughout life, till (with luck) death from old age. This theory underlies all the various schools of psychology and provides a useful agreed principle. We may differ violently here and there, but this simple idea of continuity of emotional growth joins us all together. From this base we can study

146

the manner of the process, and the various stages at which there is danger, either from within (instincts) or from without (environmental failure).

We all accept the general statement that the earlier we go in the examination of this process of individual growth, the more important we find the environmental factor. This is an acceptance of the principle that the child goes from dependence towards independence. In health we expect the individual to become gradually able to identify with wider and wider groups, and to identify with groups without loss of sense of self and of individual spontaneity. If the group is too wide the individual loses touch; if it is too narrow there is a loss of sense of citizenship.

We take much trouble to provide *gradual* extensions of the meaning of the word group in our provision of clubs and other organizations suitable for adolescents, and we judge success by the way in which each boy or girl can identify with each group in succession, without too great a loss of individuality. For the pre-adolescent we provide scouts and guides; for the latency child, cubs and brownies. At the first school age, school gives an extension and a widening of the home. If school is to be provided for the toddler then we see that it is integrated in with the home, and that it does not place too much value on actual teaching, because what a toddler needs is organized opportunity for play and controlled conditions for the beginnings of a social life. For the toddler we recognize that the true group is the child's own home, and for the infant we know that it is a disaster if a break in the continuity of home management becomes necessary. If we look at the earlier stages of this process we see the infant very dependent on the mother's management, and on her continued presence and her survival. She must make a good-enough adaptation to the infant's needs, else the infant cannot avoid developing defences that distort the process; for instance, the infant must take over the environmental function if the environment is not reliable, so that there is a hidden true self, and all that we can see is a false self engaged in the double task of hiding the true self and of complying with the demands that the world makes from moment to moment.

Still earlier, the infant is held by the mother, and only understands love that is expressed in physical terms, that is to say, by live, human holding. Here is absolute dependence, and environmental failure at this very early stage cannot be defended against, except by a hold-up of the developmental process, and by infantile psychosis.

Let us look now at what happens when the environment behaves well enough, all along well enough according to the needs that are specific to the moment. Psycho-analysis concerns itself (and it must do so) primarily with the meeting of instinctual needs (the ego and the id), but in this context we are more concerned with the environmental provision that makes all the rest possible; that is to say, we are more concerned here and now with the mother *holding* the baby than with the mother *feeding* the baby. What do we find in the process of individual emotional growth when the holding and the general management are good enough?

Of all that we find, that which chiefly concerns us here is that part of the process which we call integration. Before integration the individual is unorganized, a mere collection of sensory-motor phenomena, collected by the holding environment. After integration the individual IS, that is to say, the infant human being has achieved unit status, can say I AM (except for not being able to talk). The individual has now a limiting membrane, so that what is not-he or not-she is repudiated, and is external. The he or the she has now an inside, and here can be collected memories of experiences, and can be built up the infinitely complex structure that belongs to the human being.

It does not matter if this development happens in a moment or gradually over a long period of time; the fact is that there is a before and an after, and the process deserves a name all to itself.

No doubt the instinctual experiences contribute richly to the integration process, but there is also all the time the good-enough environment, someone holding the infant, and adapting well enough to changing needs. That someone cannot function except through the sort of love that is appropriate at this stage, love that carries a capacity for identification with the infant, and a feeling that adaptation to need is worth while. We say that the mother is devoted to her infant, temporarily but truly. She likes to be preoccupied in this way, until the need for her wanes.

I suggest that this I AM moment is a raw moment; the new individual feels infinitely exposed. Only if someone has her arms round the infant at this time can the I AM moment be endured, or rather, perhaps, risked.

I would add that at this moment it is convenient when the psyche and the body have the same places in space, so that the limiting membrane is not only metaphorically a limit to the psyche, but also it is the skin of the body. 'Exposed' then means 'naked'.

Before integration there is a state in which the individual only exists for those who observe. For the infant the external world is not differentiated out, nor is there an inner or personal world or an inner reality. After integration the infant begins to have a self. Whereas before, what the mother can do is to be ready to be repudiated, afterwards what she can do is to supply support, warmth, loving care, and clothes (and soon she starts catering for instincts).

Also in this period before integration there is an area between the mother and the infant that is *both* mother and infant. If all goes well, this very gradually splits into two elements, the part that the infant eventually repudiates and the part that the infant eventually claims. But we must expect relics of this intermediate area to persist. We do indeed see this later in the infant's first affectionately held possession – perhaps a bit of cloth derived from a blanket, bedcover, or shirt; or a napkin, mother's handkerchief, etc. Such an object I like to call a 'transitional object', and the point of it is that it is both (and at the same time) a creation of the infant and a part of external reality. For this reason parents respect this object even more than they do the teddies and dolls and toys that quickly follow. The baby who loses the transitional object at the same time loses both mouth and breast, both hand and mother's skin, both creativity and objective perception. The object is one of the bridges that make contact possible between the individual psyche and external reality.

In the same way it is unthinkable that an infant should exist, before integration, without good-enough mothering. Only after integration can we say that if the mother fails the infant dies of cold, or falls infinitely down, or flies off and away, or bursts like a hydrogen bomb and destroys the self and the world in one and the same moment.

The newly integrated infant is, then, in the first *group*. Before this stage there is only a primitive pre-group formation, in which unintegrated elements are held together by an environment from which they are not yet differentiated This environment is the holding mother.

A group is an I AM achievement, and it is a dangerous achievement. In the initial stages protection is needed, else the repudiated external world comes back at the new phenomenon and attacks from all quarters and in every conceivable way.

If we continued this study of the individual's evolution, we would see how the more and more complex personal growth complicates the picture of group growth. But at this point let us follow up the implications of our basic assumption.

THE FORMATION OF GROUPS

We have reached the stage of *an integrated human unit*, and at the same time someone who might be called *mother who supplies covering*, knowing full well the paranoid state that is inherent in the newly integrated state. I can hope to be understood if I use the two terms 'individual unit' and 'maternal covering'.

Groups may have origin in either of the two extremes implied in these terms:

 (i) Superimposed units
 (ii) Covering.

(i) The basis of mature group formation is the multiplication of individual units. Ten persons, who are personally well integrated, loosely superimpose their ten integrations and to some degree share a limiting membrane. The limiting membrane is now representative of the skin of each individual mem-

149

ber. The organization that each individual brings in terms of personal integration tends to maintain the group entity from within. This means that the group benefits from the personal experience of the individuals, each of whom has been seen through the integration moment, and has been covered until able to provide self-cover.

The group's integration implies at first an expectation of persecution, and for this reason persecution of a certain type can artificially produce a group formation, but not a stable group formation.

(ii) At the other extreme a collection of relatively unintegrated persons can be given covering, and a group may be formed. Here the group work does not come from the individuals but from the covering. The individuals go through three stages:

(*a*) They are glad to be covered and they gain confidence.

(*b*) They begin to exploit the situation, becoming dependent, and regressing to unintegration.

(*c*) They begin, independently of each other, to achieve some integration, and at such times they use the cover offered by the group which they need because of their expectation of persecution. Great strain is placed on the cover mechanisms. Some of these individuals do achieve personal integration, and so become ready to be moved to the other type of group in which the individuals themselves provide the group work. Others cannot be cured by cover-therapy alone, and they continue to need to be managed by an agency without identification with that agency.

It is possible to see which extreme predominates in any one group that is examined. The word 'democracy' is used to describe the most mature grouping, and democracy only applies to a collection of adult persons of whom the vast majority have achieved personal integration (as well as being mature in other ways).

Adolescent groups may achieve a kind of democracy under supervision. It is a mistake, however, to expect democracy to ripen among adolescents, even when each individual is mature. With younger healthy children the cover aspect of any group must be in evidence, while every chance is given to the individuals to contribute to the group cohesion through the same forces that promote cohesion within the individual ego structures. The limited group gives opportunity for individual contribution.

GROUP WORK WITH THE MALADJUSTED CHILD

The study of group formations composed of healthy adults, adolescents, or children throws light on the problem of group management where the children are ill, illness here meaning maladjusted.

This ugly word – maladjustment – means that at some early date the environment failed to adjust appropriately to the child, and the child is therefore compelled either to take over the cover-work and so to lose personal identity, or else to push round in society forcing someone else to act cover, so that a chance may come for a new start with personal integration.

The antisocial child has two alternatives – to annihilate the true self or to shake society up till it provides cover. In the second alternative if cover is found then the true self can re-emerge, and it is better to exist in prison than to become annihilated in meaningless compliance.

In terms of the two extremes that I have described, it is evident that no group of maladjusted children will adhere because of the personal integration of the boys and girls. This is partly due to the fact that the group is composed of adolescents or children, immature human beings, but chiefly because the children are all more or less unintegrated. Each boy or girl therefore has an abnormal degree of need for cover because each is ill in just that way, having been overstrained in this matter of the integration process at some point or other in early childhood or in infancy.

How, then, can we provide for these children in such a way as to ensure that what we offer them will be adapted to their changing needs as they progress towards health? There are two alternative methods:

(i) By the first, a hostel keeps the same group of children and is responsible for seeing them through; it provides what is necessary at the various stages of their development. In the beginning the staff provide cover, and the group is a cover-group. In this cover-group the children (after the honeymoon period) become worse, and with luck they reach a rock-bottom of unintegration. They do not all do this at one moment, fortunately, and they use each other, so that one child is usually much worse than the others at any one time. (How tempting it is to be always getting rid of the one, and so to be always failing at the critical point!)

Gradually one by one the children begin to achieve personal integration, and in the course of five to ten years they are the same children but they have become a new kind of group. Cover technique can be lessened, and the group starts to integrate by the forces that make for integration within each individual.

The staff are always ready to re-establish cover, as when a child steals in the first job, or in some other way shows symptoms of the fear that belongs to a belated attainment of the I AM state, or relative independence.

(ii) By the other method, a group of hostels work together. Each hostel is classified according to the kind of work it is doing, and it maintains its type. For example:

A hostel gives 100 per cent cover
B hostel gives 90 per cent cover
C hostel gives 65 per cent cover
D hostel gives 50 per cent cover
E hostel gives 40 per cent cover

The children know the various hostels in the group through visits that are deliberately planned, and there are interchanges of assistants also. When a child in A hostel achieves some sort of personal integration he or she moves up one. In this way the children who improve progress towards E hostel, which is able to cover the child's adolescent plunge into the world.

The group of hostels is itself covered, in such a case, by some authority and by a hostels committee.

The awkward thing about this second method is that the hostel staffs will fail to understand each other unless they meet and are kept fully informed as to the method employed and the way it is working out. The B hostel that gives 90 per cent cover and does all the dirty work will be looked down on; there will be alarms and excursions at this hostel. Hostel A will be better placed because here there will be no room at all for individual freedom; all the children will look happy and well fed, and visitors will like it the best of all the five. The warden will need to be a dictator and he will no doubt think that the failures in the other hostels are due to lax discipline. But the children in Hostel A have not yet started. They are getting ready to start.

In Hostels B and C, where children lie about on the floor, cannot get up, refuse to eat, mess their pants, steal whenever they feel a loving impulse, torture cats, kill mice and bury them so as to have a cemetery where they can go and cry, in these hostels there should be a notice: visitors not admitted. The wardens of these hostels have the perpetual job of covering naked souls, and they see as much suffering as can be seen in a mental hospital for adults. How difficult it is to keep a good staff under these conditions!

SUMMARY

Of all that can be said about hostels as groups I have chosen to speak of the relation of the group work to the plus or minus quantity of the personal integration of the individual children. I believe this relationship to be basic: where there is a plus sign the children bring their own integrating forces with them; when there is a minus sign the hostel provides cover, like clothes for a naked child and like the personal human holding of an infant newly born.

When there is a muddle of classification in respect of the factor of personal integration, then a hostel cannot find its place. The illnesses of the ill children dominate, and the more normal children who could be contributing to the group work cannot be given opportunity, since cover must be provided all the time and everywhere.

I believe that my over-simplification of the problem in this way will be justified if it can give a simple language for the better classification of children and of hostels. Those who work in such hostels are being all the time avenged for innumerable early environmental failures which were not their doing. If they are to stand the terrific strain of tolerating this and even in some cases of correcting the past failure through their tolerance, then they must at least know what it is that they are doing, and why it is that they cannot all the time succeed.

CLASSIFICATION OF CASES

On the basis of acceptance of the ideas that have been put forward, it is possible gradually to enter into the complexity of the problem of groups. I conclude with a rough classification of types of case.

(a) Those children who are ill in the sense that they have not become integrated into units, and who therefore cannot contribute to a group.

(b) Those children who have developed a false self which has the function of making and maintaining contact with the environment and at the same time of protecting and hiding the true self. In these cases there is a deceptive integration which breaks down as soon as it is taken for granted and called upon for a contribution.

(c) Those children who are ill in the sense of being withdrawn. Here the integration has been achieved and the defence is along the lines of a rearrangement of benign and malign forces. These children live in their own inner worlds which are artificially benign although alarming because of the operation of magic. Their outer worlds are malign or persecutory.

(d) Those children who maintain a personal integration by over-emphasis of integration, and a defence from threat of disintegration which takes the form of establishment of a strong personality.

(e) Those children who have known good-enough early management and who have been able to employ an intermediate world with objects that derive importance through representing at one and the same time external and internal objects of value. They have nevertheless suffered from an interruption of the continuity of their management to a degree which broke up the use of intermediate objects. These children are the ordinary 'deprived complex' children, whose behaviour develops antisocial qualities whenever they begin to hope again. They steal and crave for affection and claim that we shall believe their lies. At their best they regress in a general way, or in a localized way as in bed-wetting, which represents a momentary regression in relation to a dream. At their worst they force society to tolerate their symptoms of hope although they are unable immediately to benefit from their symptoms. They do not find what they want by stealing but they may eventually (because someone tolerates their stealing) reach some degree of new belief in having a claim on the world. In this group is the whole range of antisocial behaviour.

(*f*) Those children who have had a tolerably good early start but who suffer from the effects of parental figures with whom it is unsuitable for them to identify. There are innumerable subgroups here, examples of which are:

   (i) Mother chaotic
  (ii) Mother depressed
 (iii) Father absent
  (iv) Mother anxious
   (v) Father appearing as stern parent without earning the right to be stern
  (vi) Parents quarrelling, which joins up with overcrowded conditions and the child sleeping in the parents' room, etc.

(*g*) Children with manic-depressive tendencies, with or without a hereditary or genetic element.

(*h*) Children who are normal except when in depressive phases.

(*i*) Children with an expectation of persecution and a tendency to get bullied or to become bullies. In boys this can form the basis of homosexual practice.

(*j*) Children who are hypomanic, with the depression either latent or hidden in psychosomatic disorders.

(*k*) All those children who are sufficiently integrated and socialized to suffer (when they are ill) from the inhibitions and compulsions and organizations of defence against anxiety, which are roughly classed together under the word psychoneurosis.

(*l*) Lastly, the normal children, by which we mean children who, when faced with environmental abnormalities or danger situations, can employ any defence mechanism, but who are not driven towards one type of defence mechanism by distortions of personal emotional development.

[1950

18

Some Thoughts on the Meaning
of the Word Democracy

First of all let me say that I realize I am offering comments on a subject that is outside my own speciality. Sociologists and political scientists may at first resent this impertinence. Yet it seems to me to be valuable for workers to cross the boundaries from time to time, provided that they realize (as I do indeed) that their remarks must inevitably appear naïve to those who know the relevant literature and who are accustomed to a professional language of which the intruder is ignorant.

This word *democracy* has great importance at the present time. It is used in all sorts of different senses; here are a few:

  (i) A social system in which the people rule.
 (ii) A social system in which the people choose the leader.
(iii) A social system in which people choose the government.
(iv) A social system in which the government allows the people freedom of:
    (*a*) thought and expression of opinion,
    (*b*) enterprise.
 (v) A social system which, being on a run of good fortune, can afford to allow individuals freedom of action.

One can study:

  (i) The etymology of the word.
 (ii) The history of social institutions, Greek, Roman, etc.
(iii) The use made of the word by various countries and cultures at the present time, Great Britain, the United States, Russia, etc.
(iv) The abuse of the word by dictators and others; hoodwinking the people, etc.

In any discussion on a term, such as democracy, it is obviously of first importance that a definition should be reached, suitable for the particular type of discussion.

Psychology of the Use of the Term

Is it possible to study the use of this term psychologically? We accept and are accustomed to psychological studies of other difficult terms such as 'normal mind', 'healthy personality', 'individual well-adjusted to society', and we expect such studies to prove valuable in so far as they give unconscious emotional factors their full import. One of the tasks of psychology is to study and present the latent ideas that exist in the use of such concepts, not confining attention to obvious or conscious meaning.

An attempt is made here to initiate a psychological study.

Working Definition of the Term

It does seem that an important latent meaning of this term can be found, namely, that a democratic society is 'mature', that is to say, that it has a quality that is allied to the quality of individual maturity which characterizes its healthy members.

Democracy is here defined, therefore, as 'society well-adjusted to its *healthy* individual members'. This definition is in accord with the view expressed by R. E. Money-Kyrle (Mental Health Congress, 1948 Bulletin).

It is the way people use this term that is important to the psychologist. A psychological study is justified if there is implied in the term the element of *maturity*. The suggestion is that in all uses of the term there can be found to be implied the idea of maturity or relative maturity, though it is difficult, as all will admit, to define these terms adequately.

Psychiatric Health

In psychiatric terms, the normal or healthy individual can be said to be one who is mature; according to his or her chronological age and social setting there is an appropriate degree of emotional development. (In this argument physical maturity is assumed.)

Psychiatric health is therefore a term without fixed meaning. In the same way the term 'democratic' need not have a fixed meaning. Used by a community it may mean *the more rather than the less mature in society structure*. In this way one would expect the frozen meaning of the word to be different in Great Britain, the United States, and the Soviet Union, and yet to find that the term retains value because of its implying the recognition of maturity as health.

How can one study the emotional development of society? Such a study must be closely related to the study of the individual. The two studies must take place simultaneously.

DEMOCRATIC MACHINERY

An attempt must be made to state the accepted qualities of democratic machinery. The machinery must exist for the *election* of leaders by free vote, true secret ballot. The machinery must exist for the people *to get rid of* leaders by secret ballot. The machinery must exist for the *illogical* election and removal of leaders.

The essence of democratic machinery is the free vote (secret ballot). The point of this is that it ensures the freedom of the people to express deep feelings, *apart from conscious thoughts.*[1]

In the exercise of the secret vote, the whole responsibility for action is taken by the individual, if he is healthy enough to take it. The vote expresses the outcome of the struggle within himself, the external scene having been internalized and so brought into association with the interplay of forces in his own personal inner world. That is to say, the decision as to which way to vote is the expression of a solution of a struggle within himself. The process seems to be somewhat as follows. The external scene, with its many social and political aspects, is made personal for him in the sense that he gradually identifies himself with all the parties to the struggle. This means that he perceives the external scene in terms of his own internal struggle, and he temporarily allows his internal struggle to be waged in terms of the external political scene. This to-and-fro process involves work and takes time, and it is part of democratic machinery to arrange for a period of preparation. A sudden election would produce an acute sense of frustration in the electorate. Each voter's inner world has to be turned into a political arena over a limited period.

If there is doubt about the secrecy of the ballot, the individual, however healthy, can only express by his vote his *reactions*.

Imposed Democratic Machinery

It would be possible to take a community and to impose on it the machinery that belongs to democracy, but this would not be to create a democracy. Someone would be needed to continue to maintain the machinery (for secret ballot, etc.), and also to force the people to accept the results.

INNATE DEMOCRATIC TENDENCY

A democracy is an achievement, at a point of time, of a limited society, i.e. of a society that has some natural boundary. Of a true democracy (as the term is used today) one can say: *In this society at this time there is sufficient maturity in the emotional development of a sufficient proportion of the in-*

---

[1] In this respect proportional representation is anti-democratic, even when secret, because it interferes with free expression of *feelings*, and it is only suitable for specialized conditions in which clever and educated people wish for a test of *conscious* opinions.

s that comprise it for there to exist an innate[1] tendency towards the
~~~ in and re-creation and maintenance of the democratic machinery.

It would be important to know what proportion of mature individuals is necessary if there is to be an innate democratic tendency. In another way of expressing this, what proportion of antisocial individuals can a society contain without submergence of innate democratic tendency?

Supposition

If the second world war, and the evacuation scheme in particular, increased the proportion of antisocial children in Great Britain from X cent to, say, $5X$ per cent, this could easily have affected the education system, so that the educational orientation was towards the $5X$ per cent antisocials, crying out for dictatorship methods, and away from the $100—5X$ per cent children who were not antisocial.

A decade later this problem would be stated in this way, that, whereas society could cope with X per cent criminals by segregation of them in prisons, $5X$ per cent of them would tend to produce a general reorientation towards criminals.

Immature Identification with Society

In a society at any one time, if there is X quantity of individuals who show their lack of sense of society by developing an antisocial tendency, there is Z quantity of individuals reacting to inner insecurity by the alternative tendency – identification with authority. This is unhealthy, immature, because it is not an identification with authority that arises out of self-discovery. It is a sense of frame without sense of picture, a sense of form without retention of spontaneity. This is a pro-society tendency that is anti-individual. People who develop in this way can be called 'hidden antisocials'.

Hidden antisocials are not 'whole persons' any more than are manifest antisocials, since each needs to find and to control the conflicting force in the external world outside the self. By contrast, the healthy person, who is capable of becoming depressed, is able to find the whole conflict within the self as well as being able to see the whole conflict outside the self, in external (shared) reality. When healthy persons come together they each contribute a whole world, because each brings a whole person.

'Hidden antisocials' provide material for a type of leadership which is sociologically immature. Moreover, this element in a society greatly

[1] By 'innate' I intend to convey the following: the natural tendencies in human nature (hereditary) bud and flower into the democratic way of life (social maturity), but this only happens through the healthy emotional development of individuals; only a proportion of individuals in a social group will have had the luck to develop to maturity and therefore it is only through them that the innate (inherited) tendency of the group towards social maturity can be implemented.

strengthens the danger that derives from its frank antisocial elements, especially since ordinary people so easily let those with an urge to lead get into key positions. Once in such positions, these immature leaders immediately gather to themselves the obvious antisocials, who welcome them (the immature anti-individual leaders) as their natural masters. (False resolution of splitting.)

The Indeterminates
It is never as simple as this, because if there are $(X+Z)$ per cent antisocial individuals in a community, it is not true to say that $100—(X+Z)$ per cent are 'social'. There are those in an indeterminate position. One could put it:

Antisocials	X per cent
Indeterminates	Y per cent
Pro-society but anti-individual	Z per cent
Healthy individuals capable of social contribution	$100—(X+Y+Z)$ per cent
Total	100 per cent

The whole democratic burden falls on the $100—(X+Y+Z)$ per cent of individuals who are maturing as individuals, and who are gradually becoming able to add a social sense to their well-grounded personal development.

What percentage does $100—(X+Y+Z)$ per cent represent, for instance, in Great Britain today? Possibly it is quite small, say 30 per cent. Perhaps, if there are 30 per cent mature persons, as many as 20 per cent of the indeterminates will be sufficiently influenced to be counted as mature, thus bringing the total to 50 per cent. If, however, the mature percentage should drop to 20, it must be expected that there will be a bigger fall in the percentage of indeterminates able to act in a mature way. If 30 per cent maturity in a community collects 20 per cent indeterminates, i.e. a total of 50 per cent, perhaps 20 per cent maturity in a community collects only 10 per cent indeterminates, i.e. a total of 30 per cent.

Whereas a 50 per cent total might indicate sufficient innate democratic tendency for practical purposes, 30 per cent could not be counted sufficient to avoid submergence by the sum of the antisocials (hidden and manifest) and the indeterminates who would be drawn by weakness or fear into association with them.

There follows an anti-democratic tendency, a tendency towards dictatorship, characterized at first by a feverish bolstering up of the democratic façade (hoodwinking function of the term).

One sign of this tendency is the corrective institution, the localized dictatorship, the practising ground for the personally-immature leaders who are reversed antisocials (pro-social but anti-individual).

This, the corrective institution, has both the prison and the mental hospital of a healthy society perilously near to it, and for this reason the doctors of criminals and of the insane have to be constantly on guard lest they find themselves being used, without at first knowing it, as agents of the anti-democratic tendency. There must, in fact, always be a borderline in which there is no clear distinction between the corrective treatment of the political or ideational opponent and the therapy of the insane person. (Here lies the social danger of physical methods of therapy of the mental patient, as compared with true psychotherapy, or even the acceptance of a state of insanity. In psychotherapy the patient is a person on equal terms with the doctor, with a right to be ill, and also a right to claim health and full responsibility for personal political or ideational views.)

CREATION OF INNATE DEMOCRATIC FACTOR

If democracy is maturity, and maturity is health, and health is desirable, then we wish to see whether anything can be done to foster it. Certainly it will not help to impose democratic machinery on a country.

We must turn to the $100-(X+Y+Z)$ group of individuals. All depends on them. Members of this group can instigate research.

We find that at any one time we can do nothing to increase the quantity of this innate democratic factor comparable in importance to what has already been done (or not done) by the parents and homes of these individuals when they were infants and children and adolescents.

We can, however, try to avoid compromising the future. We can try to avoid interfering with the homes that can cope, and are actually coping, with their own individual children and adolescents. These *ordinary good homes* provide the only setting in which the innate democratic factor can be created.[1] This is indeed a modest statement of positive contribution, but there is a surprising amount of complexity in its application.

Factors Adverse to the Functioning of the Ordinary Good Home
(i) It is very difficult for people to recognize that the essential of a democracy really does lie with the ordinary man and woman, and the ordinary, commonplace home.

(ii) Even if a wise government policy gives parents freedom to run their homes in their own way, it is not certain that officials putting official policies into practice will respect the parents' position.

---

[1] The ordinary good home is something that defies statistical investigation. It has no news value, is not spectacular, and does not produce the men and women whose names are publicly known. My assumption, based on 20,000 case histories taken personally over a period of twenty-five years, is that in the community in which I work the ordinary good home is common, even usual.

(iii) Ordinary good parents do need help. They need all that science can offer in respect of physical health and the prevention and treatment of physical disease; also they want instruction in child care, and help when their children have psychological illnesses or present behaviour problems. But, if they seek such assistance, can they be sure they will not have their responsibilities lifted from them? If this happens they cease to be creators of the innate democratic factor.

(iv) Many parents are not ordinary good parents. They are psychiatric cases, or they are immature, or they are antisocial in a wide sense, and socialized only in a restricted sense; or they are unmarried, or in unstable relationship, or bickering, or separated from each other, and so on. These parents get attention from society, because of their defects. The thing is, can society see that the orientation towards these pathological features must not be allowed to affect society's orientation towards the ordinary healthy homes?

(v) In any case, the parents' attempt to provide a home for their children, in which the children can grow as individuals, and each *gradually add* a capacity to identify with the parents and then with wider groupings, starts at the beginning, when the mother comes to terms with her infant. Here the father is the protecting agent who frees the mother to devote herself to her baby.

The place of the home has long been recognized, and in recent years a great deal has been found out by psychologists as to the ways in which a stable home not only enables children to find themselves and to find each other, but also makes them begin to qualify for membership of society in a wider sense.

This matter of interference with the early infant-mother relationship, however, needs some special consideration. In our society there is increasing interference at this point, and there is extra danger from the fact that some psychologists actually claim that at the beginning it is only physical care that counts. This can only mean that in the unconscious fantasy of people in general the most awful ideas cluster round the infant-mother relationship. Anxiety in the unconscious is represented in practice by:

(*a*) Overemphasis by physicians and even by psychologists on *physical* processes and health.

(*b*) Various theories that breast-feeding is bad, that the baby must be trained as soon as born, that babies should not be handled by their mothers, etc.; and (in the negative) that breast-feeding *must* be established, that no training whatever should be given, that babies should never be allowed to cry, etc.

(*c*) Interference with the mother's access to her baby in the first days, and with her first presentation of external reality to the infant. This, after all, is the basis of the new individual's capacity eventually to become related to ever-widening external reality, and if the mother's tremendous contribution, *through her being devoted*, is spoilt or prevented, there is no hope that the individual will pass eventually into the $100-(X+Y+Z)$ group that alone generates the innate democratic factor.

DEVELOPMENT OF SUBSIDIARY THEMES: ELECTION OF PERSONS

Another essential part of the democratic machinery is that it is a *person* who is elected. There is all the difference in the world between (i) the vote for a person, (ii) the vote for a party with a set tendency, and (iii) the support of a clear-cut principle by ballot.

(i) The election of a person implies that the electors believe in themselves as persons, and therefore believe in the person they nominate or vote for. The person elected has the opportunity to act as a person. As a whole (healthy) person he has the total conflict within, which enables him to get a view, albeit a personal one, of total external situations. He may, of course, belong to a party and be known to have a certain tendency. Nevertheless, he can adapt in a delicate way to changing conditions; if he actually changes his main tendency he can put himself up for re-election.

(ii) The election of a party or a group tendency is relatively less mature. It does not require of the electors a trust in a human being. For immature persons, nevertheless, it is the only logical procedure, precisely because an immature person cannot conceive of, or believe in, a truly mature individual. The result of the vote for a party or tendency, for a thing and not a person, is the establishment of a rigid outlook, ill-adapted for delicate reactions. This *thing* that is elected cannot be loved or hated, and it is suitable for individuals who have a poorly developed sense of self. It could be said that a system of voting is less democratic, because less mature (in terms of emotional development of the individual), when the accent is on the vote for the principle or party and not on the vote for the person.

(iii) Much further removed from anything associated with the word democracy is the ballot on a specific point. There is little of maturity about a referendum (although this can be made to fit in with a mature system on exceptional occasions). As an example of the way in which a referendum is un-useful can be cited the peace ballot, between the two world wars, in Great Britain. People were asked to answer a specific question ('Are you in favour of peace or war?'). A large number of people abstained from voting because they knew that the question was an unfair one. Of those who voted a big proportion put their crosses against the word peace, although in actual fact, when circumstances rearranged themselves, they were in favour of the war when it came, and took part in the fighting. The point is that in this type of questioning there is only room for the expression of the *conscious* wish. There is no relation between putting one's tick against the word 'peace' in such a ballot and voting for a person who is known to be eager for peace provided the failure to fight does not mean a lazy abandonment of aspirations and responsibilities and the betrayal of friends.

The same objection applies to much of the Gallup Poll and other question-naires, even although a great deal of trouble is taken to avoid exactly this pitfall. In any case, a vote on a specific point is a very poor substitute indeed for the vote in favour of a person who, once elected, has a space of time in which he can use his own judgement. The referendum has nothing to do with democracy.

SUPPORT OF DEMOCRATIC TENDENCY: SUMMARY

1. The most valuable support is given in a negative way by organized non-interference with the ordinary good mother-infant relationship, and with the ordinary good home.

2. For more intelligent support, even of this negative kind, much research is needed on the emotional development of the infant and the child of all ages, and also on the psychology of the nursing mother and of the father's function at various stages.

3. The existence of this study shows a belief in the value of education in democratic procedure, which of course can only be given in so far as there is understanding, and can only be usefully given to the emotionally mature or healthy individuals.

4. Another important negative contribution would be the avoidance of attempts to implant democratic machinery on total communities. The result can only be failure, and a setback to true democratic growth. The alternative and valuable action is to support the emotionally mature individuals, however few they may be, and to let time do the rest.

PERSON – MAN OR WOMAN?

The point that has to be considered is whether in the place of the word 'person' there can be put 'man' or 'woman'.

The fact is that the political heads of most countries are men, although women are increasingly used for responsible posts. It can perhaps be assumed that men and women have an equal capacity *qua* men and women; or, the other way round, it would not be possible to say that only men could be suitable for leadership on grounds of intellectual or emotional capacity for the highest political post. Nevertheless, this does not dispose of the problem. It is the psychologist's task to draw attention to the *unconscious* factors which are easily left out of account, even in serious discussions on this sort of subject. The thing that has to be considered is unconscious popular feeling in regard to the man or woman who is elected to the position of political chief. If there is a difference in the fantasy according to whether it be a man or a woman, this cannot be ignored, nor can it be brushed aside by the comment that fantasies ought not to count because they are 'only fantasies'.

In psycho-analytical and allied work it is found that all individuals (men and women) have in reserve a certain fear of *woman*.[1] Some individuals have this fear to a greater extent than others, but it can be said to be universal. This is quite different from saying that an individual fears a particular woman. This fear of *woman* is a powerful agent in society structure, and it is responsible for the fact that in very few societies does a woman hold the political reins. It is also responsible for the immense amount of cruelty to women, which can be found in customs that are accepted by almost all civilizations.

The root of this fear of *woman* is known. It is related to the fact that in the early history of every individual who develops well, and who is sane, and who has been able to find himself, there is a debt to a woman – the woman who was devoted to that individual as an infant, and whose devotion was absolutely essential for that individual's healthy development. The original dependence is not remembered, and therefore the debt is not acknowledged, except in so far as the fear of *woman* represents the first stage of this acknowledgement.

The foundation of the mental health of the individual is laid down at the very beginning when the mother is simply being devoted to her infant and when the infant is doubly dependent because totally unaware of dependence. There is no relation to the father which has such a quality, and for this reason a man who in a political sense is at the top can be appreciated by the group much more objectively than a woman can be if she is in a similar position.

Women often claim that if women were in charge of affairs there would be no wars. There are reasons why this may be doubted as a final statement of

---

[1] It would be out of place to discuss this here in detail, but the idea can be reached best if approached gradually:

(i) Fear of the parents of very early childhood.

(ii) Fear of a combined figure, a woman with male potency included in her powers (witch).

(iii) Fear of the mother who had absolute power at the beginning of the infant's existence to provide, or to fail to provide, the essentials for the early establishment of the self as an individual.

This is further discussed in 'The Mother's Contribution to Society', the Postscript to *The Child and the Family* by D. W. Winnicott (London: Tavistock Publications, 1957); and in the Introduction to *The Child, the Family, and the Outside World* by D. W. Winnicott (Harmondsworth: Penguin Books, 1964).

truth, but, even if the claim were justified, it would still not follow that men or women would ever tolerate the general principle of women generally at the highest points of political power. (The Crown, by being outside or beyond politics, is not affected by these considerations.)

As an offshoot of this consideration, one can consider the psychology of the dictator, who is at the opposite pole to anything that the word democracy can mean. *One of the roots of the need to be dictator can be a compulsion to deal with this fear of woman by encompassing her and acting for her.* The dictator's curious habit of demanding not only absolute obedience and absolute dependence but also 'love' can be derived from this source.

Moreover, the tendency of groups of people to accept or even seek *actual* domination is derived from a fear of domination by *fantasy woman*. This fear leads them to seek, and even welcome, domination by a known human being, especially one who has taken on himself the burden of personifying and therefore limiting the magical qualities of the all-powerful woman of fantasy, to whom is owed the great debt. The dictator can be overthrown, and must eventually die; but the woman figure of primitive unconscious fantasy has no limits to her existence or power.

CHILD-PARENT RELATIONSHIP

The democratic set-up includes the provision of a certain degree of stability for the elected rulers; as long as they can manage their job without alienating the support of their electors, they carry on. In this way the people arrange for a certain amount of stability which they could not maintain through direct voting on every point, even if that were possible. The psychological consideration here is that there is in the history of every individual the fact of the parent-child relationship. Although in the mature democratic way of political life the electors are presumably mature human beings, it cannot be assumed that there is no place for a residue of the parent-child relationship, with its obvious advantages. To some extent, in the democratic election mature people elect temporary parents, which means that they also acknowledge the fact that to some extent the electors remain children. Even the elected temporary parents, the rulers of the democratic political system, are children themselves outside their professional political work. If in driving their cars they exceed the speed limit they come under ordinary judicial censure because driving a car is not part of their job of ruling. As political leaders, and only as such, they are temporarily parents, and after being deposed at an election they revert to being children. It is as if it is convenient to play a game of parents and children because things work out better that way. In other words, because there are advantages in the parent-child relationship, some of this is retained; but, for this to be possible, a sufficient proportion of individuals need to be grown-up enough not to mind playing at being children.

In the same way, it is thought to be bad for these people who are playing at parents to have no parents themselves. In the game it is generally thought that there should be another house of representatives to which the rulers who are directly elected by the people should be responsible. In this country this function belongs to the House of Lords, which is to some extent composed of those who have a hereditary title, and to some extent of those who have won a position there by eminence in various branches of public work. Once again the 'parents' of the 'parents' are persons, and capable of making positive contributions as human beings. And it makes sense to love or to hate or to respect or to despise persons. There can be no substitute in a society for the human beings or being at the top, in so far as that society is to be rated according to its quality of emotional maturity.

And further, in a study of the social setting in Great Britain, we can see that the lords are children, relative to the Crown. Here in each case we come again to a person, who holds his or her position by heredity, and also by maintaining the love of the people by his or her personality and actions. It is certainly helpful when the reigning monarch quite easily and sincerely carries the matter a stage further and proclaims a belief in God. Here we reach the interrelated subjects of The Dying God and The Eternal Monarch.

GEOGRAPHICAL BOUNDARY OF A DEMOCRACY

For the development of a democracy, in the sense of a mature society structure, it seems that it is necessary that there should be some natural geographical boundary for that society. Obviously, up to recently and even now, the fact that Great Britain is seabound (except for its relation to Eire) has been very much responsible for the maturity of our society structure. Switzerland has (less satisfactorily) mountain limits. America till recently had the advantage of a west which offered unlimited exploitation; this meant that the United States, while being united by positive ties, did not till recently need to start to feel to the full the internal struggles of a closed community, united in spite of hate as well as because of love.

A state that has no natural frontier cannot relax an active adaptation to neighbours. In one sense, fear *simplifies* the emotional situation, for many of the indeterminate Y and some of the less severe of the antisocial X become able to identify with the state on the basis of a cohesive reaction to an external persecution threat. This simplification is detrimental, however, to the development towards maturity, which is a difficult thing, involving full acknowledgement of essential conflict, and the non-employment of any way out or way round (defences).

In any case, the basis for a society is the whole human personality, and the personality has a limit. The diagram of a healthy person is a circle (sphere), so that whatever is not-self can be described as either inside or outside that person. It is not possible for persons to get further in society-building than they can get with their own personal development.

For these reasons we regard with suspicion the use of terms like 'world citizenship'. Perhaps only a few really great and fairly aged men and women ever get as far in their own development as to be justified in thinking in such wide terms.

If the whole world were our society, then it would need to be at times in a depressed mood (as a person at times inevitably has to be), and it would have to be able fully to acknowledge essential conflict within itself. The concept of a global society brings with it the idea of the world's suicide, as well as the idea of the world's happiness. For this reason we expect the militant protagonists of the world state to be individuals who are in a manic swing of a manic-depressive psychosis.

both sides do exist in current reality

EDUCATION IN DEMOCRATIC LORE

Such democratic tendency as exists can be strengthened by a study of the psychology of social as well as of individual maturity. The results of such study must be given in understandable language to the existing democracies and to healthy individuals everywhere, so that they may become *intelligently self-conscious*. Unless they are self-conscious they cannot know what to attack and what to defend, nor can they recognize threats to democracy when these arise. 'The price of freedom is eternal vigilance'; vigilance by whom? – by two or three of the $100-(X+Y+Z)$ per cent mature individuals. The others are busy just being ordinary good parents, handing on the job of growing up, and of being grown-up, to their children.

DEMOCRACY AT WAR

The question must be asked, is there such a thing as democracy at war? The answer is certainly not a plain yes. In fact, there are some reasons why, in war-time, there should be an announcement of temporary suspension of democracy because of war.

It is clear that mature healthy individuals, collectively forming a democracy, should be able to go to war: (i) to make room to grow; (ii) to defend what is valued, already possessed, etc.; and (iii) to fight anti-democratic tendencies in so far as there are people to support such tendencies by fighting.

Nevertheless, it must be but seldom that things have worked out that way. According to the description given above, a community is never composed of 100 per cent of healthy, mature individuals.

As soon as war approaches, there is a rearrangement of groups, so that by the time war is being fought it is not the healthy who are doing all the fighting. Taking our four groups:

(a) Many of the antisocials, along with mild paranoiacs, feel better because of actual war, and they welcome the real persecution threat. They find a pro-social tendency by active fighting.

(b) Of the indeterminates, many step over into what is the thing to do, perhaps using the grim reality of war to grow up as they would not otherwise had done.

(c) Of the hidden antisocials, probably some find opportunity for the urge to dominate in the various key positions which war creates.

(d) The mature, healthy individuals do not necessarily show up as well as the others. They are not so certain as the others are that the enemy is bad. They have doubts. Also they have a bigger positive stake in the world's culture, and in beauty and in friendship, and they cannot easily believe war is necessary. Compared with the near-paranoiacs they are slow in getting the gun in hand and in pulling the trigger. In fact, they miss the bus to the front line, even if when they get there they are the reliable factor and the ones best able to adapt to adversity.

Moreover, some of the healthy of peace-time become antisocial in war (conscientious objectors), not from cowardice but from a genuine personal doubt, just as the antisocials of peace-time tend to find themselve in brave action in war.

For these and other reasons, when a democratic society is fighting, it is the whole group that fights, and it would be difficult to find an instance of a war conducted by just those of a community who provide the innate democratic factor in peace.

It may be that, when a war has disturbed a democracy, it is best to say that at that moment democracy is at an end, and those who like that way of life will have to start again and fight inside the group for the re-establishment of democratic machinery, after the end of the external conflict.

This is a large subject, and it deserves the attention of large-minded people.

SUMMARY

1. The use of the word democracy can be studied psychologically on the basis of its implication of maturity

2. Neither democracy nor maturity can be implanted on a society.

3. Democracy is an achievement of a limited society at any one time.

4. The innate democratic factor in a community derives from the working of the ordinary good home.

5. The main activity for promotion of democratic tendency is a negative one: avoidance of interference with the ordinary good home. Study of psychology and education according to what is known provide additional help.

6. There is special significance in the devotion of the ordinary good mother to her infant, the capacity for eventual emotional maturity being founded as a result of the devotion. Mass interference at this point, in a society, would quickly and effectually lessen the democratic potential of that society, just as it would diminish the richness of its culture.

Index

acting out, 92, 94
adaptation
  active, to child, 23–5
  and infant care, 4
  failure of, and mind, 7
  mother's, as enclosure, 35
  mother's, to infant's needs, 4, 89
administration, and deprived child, 137
adolescence
  antisocial tendency in, 86–7
  being defrauded of, 82, 87
  cure for, 79, 84
  defiance and dependence in, 81, 88–9,
    102–3
  delayed, in parents, 45
  depression in, 87
  discovery of self in, 79–87
  doldrums in, 85–7
  effect of social change on contemporary,
    82–3
  ego organization in, 80
  environmental provision for, 88–9
  false solution not accepted in, 84–7
  group formation in, 81–7, 150
  happenings in, 86–7
  illness patterns in, 85
  isolation in, 81–7
  masturbation in, 81
  modern and social changes in, 82–4
  needs of, 85
  need to be not understood in, 79
  rejection of cure in, 86
  security-testing in, 32–3
  suicide in 87
adoption, 135
  and deprivation, 135
  and imaginative needs, 43
advice
  and doctors, 114–15
  to parents, 114–20
  v. treatment, 114–15
aggression
  and depression, 59–60
  and destructiveness, 59–60

  and environmental failure, 12
  and motility, 12
alimentary functions, 9
ambivalence, in infancy, 104
amnesia, childhood, 35
analyst, *see* psycho-analyst
anger, and hope, in deprived child, 135–6,
  139–40
anorexia, case of girl, 73–4
antisocial tendency, 48, 64
  and adolescence, 85–7
  and authority, 64–5
  and delinquency and psychopathy, 51
  and deprivation, 14, 135–6
  and hope, 135
  and identification with society, 158
  and need for specialized environment, 136
  and psychosis, 62, 128–9
  and schools, 146
  and society 151
  and trauma from deprivation, 51
  and war, 168
anxiety
  at first maturity, 103
  at four years, 101
  expressed by society, 161–2
  intolerable, from deprivation, 136
  psychotic, from faulty holding, 18
  relating to unintegrated state, 6
artist
  and security, 33
  child as, 23
atom bomb, effect on adolescent, 83
audience, and creative capacity, 12
authority, and antisocial tendency, 64–5
auto-erotism, 42
autonomy, growth to, 88
awareness, infant's unawareness of dependence, 4

'bad', 8
bed-wetting, 136
being
  as experience in infancy, 19

171